Wakefield Press

Sourcing the Sauce

Belinda Hannaford has excelled in living and loving with a sense of humour. Her strength is always finding a way through relentless obstacles. Belinda has touched on a thousand things including singing her own compositions and entertaining, cooking, running restaurants and starting community programs. *Sourcing the Sauce* is Belinda's first book. She hopes that by sharing her life and how she lived it, others will be inspired to make sense of their world.

Sourcing the Sauce

THE CRAZY COOKBOOK OF MY LIFE

Belinda Hannaford

Wakefield
Press

Wakefield Press
16 Rose Street
Mile End
South Australia 5031
www.wakefieldpress.com.au

First published 2020

Cover designed by Liz Nicholson, Wakefield Press
Edited by Margot Lloyd, Wakefield Press
Typeset by Michael Deves, Wakefield Press

ISBN 978 1 74305 691 2

A catalogue record for this book is available from the National Library of Australia

Wakefield Press thanks Coriole Vineyards for continued support

Contents

Introduction

Sourcing the sauce is a crazy adventure, the cookbook of life.

The creative topping = the sauce
The substance of being = the source

From opulence, decadence, fame and fortune to creativity.
From creativity to mental illness.
From mental illness to mental health.
From revelation to resolution.

With a sense of humour being the icing on the cake.

CHAPTER 1

Hors d'oeuvres

In the beginning

Cooking was the only thing in my life I had control over. In this book, I have included a few recipes in Entree, Mains, and Sweets – the best of my own, but also my mother's and children's as they are all linked to my story.

DREAMS

I was seven, sitting in the tall, dry grass on the hilltop above Snelling Beach on Kangaroo Island, South Australia. 'One day I'm going to live up here and own a restaurant called Belinda's.' Thirty years later, I do live here and I have owned a restaurant called Belinda's. Hospitality has been at the heart of my life.

I grew up in the kitchen for years and years it seems,
Slurping up the sauces, licking up the creams,
Experimenting, implementing recipes untried,
With sisters all to intervene and Mama by my side.

The kitchen was my comforter with adolescent fears,
Enormous slabs of chocolate cake to wipe away my tears,
Lucky I was five foot ten and nervous as a cat,
With all that pent-up energy I couldn't turn to fat.

Frozen dinners, microwave, glad wrap, instant cake,
Where's the need to grow your own?
When's the need to bake?
Rest assured it's easier but where is all the fun?
It's just not like the good old days when cooking with my mum.

To old traditions that I knew, that now are kind of queer.
The children cook the way I did and I'm the one to sneer.
I still live in the kitchen. I'll die here I expect.
To pate, sauces and terrines, I'll pay my last respect.
The pleasures sought have been rewarded in this cutthroat game,
But for it, I would not have the slightest claim to fame!

Age: twenty-three

ROBE TERRACE

Our family home was grand. It was two storeys and a Victorian colonial hybrid, set on an acre block. The front overlooked huge parklands in an inner suburb of Adelaide. In need of a renovation, it was bought before the war by my parents for very little. When my father became managing director of General Motors Holden a deal was struck whereby the company took over the holding and provided the finance to renovate it back to its grand state – something my parents could not have afforded at that time.

The front room of the house was a huge ballroom, with a grand piano. This was our formal dining room. Opposite the front door was the 'top room', a space we occupied one by one when we 'came of age'.

Then there was the bar room (my father's domain). This room was always under his control and featured a revolving bar of his own design. It was here he spent most of his time, from the moment he arrived home at five until seven when we had dinner, returning again after dinner and staying late into the night on weekends.

There was a breakfast room for casual meals, and a nursery where we were supervised by the nannies. Nearby was the kitchen, and a tiny maid's quarters.

Up a grand staircase were five bedrooms and one bathroom. This one bathroom created a morning ritual that caused me great anxiety. I woke up every day to the sound of my father's voice bellowing down the passage to get to the bathroom – it was my turn!

PRUDENCE ELSIE STAUGHTON

My mother was born in the Western District of Victoria in 1913 into an aristocratic farming family. She was the third oldest of four girls. My school holidays were occasionally spent at Keayang, my mother's family home. Sisters and cousins joined in for family holidays. It was during those times that I really started to understand the pecking order and the rules and regulations that dominated her family, and later mine.

Children were definitely to be seen (a little) and not heard at all, so the kitchen was my mother's escape. It was a warm, cosy welcoming womb where she was nurtured by food, accepted and allowed to watch the staff, who became her friends.

Years later, my mother often expressed to me how unhappy, shy, and anxious she felt around her parents and siblings. Yet when it came to parenting us she used the same approach she'd resented so much in her own childhood.

She was a true red-haired beauty, proved by her first employment in Melbourne at age seventeen, when she was house model for Myer, and then later when she was 'discovered' after a walk-on role in one of the first Australian movies, *In Her Majesty's Secret Service*, not to be confused with the later Bond film. She so stunned the producers they then chose her for leading lady in their next film, *Diggers in Blighty*, which I did not see until I had it shown, reel-to-reel, at her seventieth birthday. The viewing was much to Mum's horror, and our fascination.

I admired my mother's presence and creativity, but I resented her inability to stand up to my father or to protect us from him. She was attentive to staff and social responsibilities, but I have no recollection of her part in my life until after I left the nursery. Even after that, my connection with her was impersonal. Except for each night at bedtime, she gave me very little physical affection.

My mother was definitely a very glamorous 'Prudence Elsie' in her early years. Then she became a bonafide 'Lady Prudence'. By the time I

My mother, Prudence Elsie, 1930

finished with her and re-programmed her after my father died, though, she grew wings with her nicknames 'Bundy' and 'Turbo'.

My parents did a lot of overseas travelling by ship just before the Second World War, and continued with interstate and shorter trips throughout my childhood, so they had little involvement in our everyday lives. The exception was Kangaroo Island, where we spent all of our school holidays, and where they were faced with us en masse.

My mother as a bikie, 1970

My father, James Holden, 1942

JAMES ROBERT HOLDEN

I would describe my father as a critical perfectionist, a man of many moods, and a disciplinarian who directed everything in his home life with a heavy hand. But there was a side of him my mother had a chance to enjoy: a generous witty side with some kind of sexual chemistry that went on behind closed doors.

My father had a huge presence; he was six feet three inches tall with blue penetrating scary eyes and a sort of Hitler-style moustache. He was an abundant man in every sense, excessive in his consumption of quality food and alcohol. Dressing immaculately in clothes ordered from London, starched and bleached, he always smelt of Tricopherous – hair oil that he splashed on half a bottle at a time. He had sock stretchers and shoetrees, and handmade handkerchiefs. His bellowing voice dominated my childhood. He taught me a work ethic, manners, respect of others and discipline, but I was terrified of his anger, physical and emotional abuse, and disapproval.

I have come to understand more about his upbringing, which helps to explain his behaviour as a parent and husband. He was born in 1903 in Turrramurra, a suburb of Sydney, and brought up in a middle-class industrial family, with two sisters, Nell and Wynn, and an older idolised brother called Leslie. Leslie could do no wrong. He was a fighter pilot in the First World War, the apple of his father's eye. He died at an early age when he crashed his plane while working for New Guinea Airways.

My father was insubordinate and rebellious in the non-drinking, religious environment of his upbringing, and he terrorised his sisters, playing terrible practical jokes on their boyfriends. He became reckless and wild, which culminated in a very bad motorbike accident that shattered his leg, ruining his chances of fighting in the Second World War. In addition, it destroyed his dream of becoming a grazier. He spent a year of convalescence, reconstruction and rehabilitation. Eventually, in retirement, he made good his vision of living on the land, and bought a sheep farm at Middle River on Kangaroo Island.

He was the black sheep of his family. His failure to launch had an enormous effect on his life from that moment on. In desperation his father asked his Uncle Henry Holden to give him a job. He started as an office dogsbody at General Motors Holden in Adelaide, though he and his cousin, who was also his boss, did not get on. From this unlikely position he succeeded eventually in becoming the managing director of the company, and was praised and admired, especially by his employees.

In midlife, he was awarded a knighthood for his efforts in making ammunition for the Second World War. Queen Elizabeth II, who was in Adelaide at that time, knighted him, and my parents became Sir James and Lady Holden. This should have been a proud moment for all of us. But deep down, I cringed at the prospect of so much more 'upper crust' rigmarole. I found out later that, even with all the public accolades, he was very unhappy in his job at General Motors.

Dad married a dancer, Mignon Keckwick, who died of septicaemia just after their first child, also called Mignon, was born. He married my mother when Mignon was five. Understandably, my mother did not find the instant stepmother role easy; neither did she plan her first child, Shylie, who was born nine months after they were married. Jill, her second daughter, was the only planned pregnancy and, sadly, Jill became the black sheep in our family, nicknamed 'Jill the Dill' by our father. I was born three years later.

Yet another daughter in a family desperate for a son.

SIBLINGS

I wish I could reflect with some sort of appreciation on my mother and father's influence in my early years, when we all lived at Robe Terrace, but for me it was a nightmare. I only realised many years later, when my mother and I moved to Kangaroo Island after Dad died, why she was unable to stand up to his tirades and protect us from harm. Her reasons were twofold: firstly, she explained how anxious and scared she had been as a child growing up in the Staughton household, where she did not have a voice; secondly, my father's alcoholism and intolerance meant if she did try and protect us, she became the target. So we children suffered physical and verbal abuse. Mignon and Shylie escaped the worst years, but even so Shylie recalls 'to try and keep my father in a good mood was really terrifying'.

In the early years, Mignon moved between her Aunt Nell in Sydney and Adelaide with nannies. Apparently, before she had a stepmother, she was taken to the Adelaide museum to see the Egyptian mummy, and was most disappointed to realise that this mummy was not meant for her. She was very happy when she finally got a mother of her own, and soon after this a baby sister. She has fond memories of the holiday times spent at Keayang with her new mummy's family.

Mignon escaped early to a live-in position at the Adelaide Children's Hospital. She became a nursing sister, married a very suitable stockbroker, whom my parents loved, and became a mother of three. Today all three children seem to have created happy, successful lives for themselves. The sudden death of her husband on retirement was a great sadness for her.

Being boys at Christmas, 1951

Shylie, my second eldest sister, seven years older than me, was blessed with very good looks. She was also sporty and creative (designing and printing Christmas cards) and extremely popular. Not only this, she was able to conform to the social and family demands put upon her by my parents, and comply to house rules and my father's dominating character. I remember her 'coming of age', and she seemed the perfect daughter and sister. Shylie was also head prefect at school.

At nineteen she was sent to be groomed by my mother's eldest sister, Lorie, who lived in rural United Kingdom. When she returned a year later, in love with a 'fine English gentleman', she slipped back into the 'upper crust', and the inner sanctum of my parents' world around the cocktail bar and social set.

I was in awe of my sister and would marvel at her long red fingernails and lipstick that matched perfectly. She wore jewel-encrusted ball gowns made by my mother and Mrs Groom, the seamstress. It seemed an idyllic life. I wanted to be like her, especially admiring her aristocratic English boyfriend, who really was in love with her. I knew this because I used to sneak to her desk and read all the wonderful and romantic letters he wrote to her.

What went wrong? It was soon to be revealed that her intended was – to my parents' shock and horror – a Roman Catholic! Catholics, blacks, Germans and Jews were a 'NO' in our family. My parents forced her to decline his marriage proposal, and I remember the night and the phone conversation from her to London. There were tears. He wrote sad love letters pleading with her to change her mind.

Finally, it all went quiet, but a few years later Shylie suddenly announced she was going to marry a penniless farmer who lived on Kangaroo Island in a run-down cottage several miles from the town of Penneshaw. He had the gift of the gab and wooed her with words. She was removed from her opulent position in our family and had to make the most of the harsh, rural lifestyle. Their marriage was a disaster from the word go. He cheated on her even before their first child was born, and they went on to have twins two years later. They finally separated many years later when he left Shylie for the 'love of his life'.

It became very clear as I reached adolescence that my sister Jill and I were the outcasts in our family. I was her ally, protector and supporter in the face of our father's wrath. Fortunately, I, like my mother before me, had friends in the kitchen as a diversion; Jill had no one but me. I did not get into quite so much trouble as she did and so survived better. She had a wretched time and became withdrawn and secretive, locking herself away in her private upstairs bedroom. She had few friends and the only two boyfriends that stood out (who were sneaked into the 'top room') were a rather dark man and a German! You can imagine how that would have gone down with my parents.

In the early years of our childhood, Jill and I were inseparable. Jill was the only thing that made my life bearable. Creativity and imagination took off. Our favourite pastimes were storytelling, dressing up, making plays and cooking. These things kept us in the moment and away from the dread of my father's choice of weapon, 'the manner whacker' – strips of leather on a stick or a rubber hose.

Suddenly, in her early twenties, Jill brought home a suitor my parents could only be delighted with. He was a university lecturer in English literature. He was handsome, charismatic but – wait for it – a lecher. Before Tony and Jill separated, their two boys became a large part of both my children's lives and mine. All the young family members created a special spot at the other end of Snelling Beach, camping out at Tolley's shack during school holidays. The adults all believed it was a safe haven and innocent fun. It proved to be otherwise. Eventually, shocking discoveries emerged that changed our family dynamics forever. The truth will be revealed later.

CHAPTER 2

Entree

I grew up in the kitchen

Smoked salmon roulade

SERVES 4

INGREDIENTS

SOUFFLÉ
4 tablespoons butter
½ cup plain flour
4 eggs separated
2 cups milk
1 pinch sugar

FILLING
½ packet Philadelphia cream cheese (room temperature)
1 small tin salmon
50 g packet smoked salmon pieces
200 g sour cream
Lemon zest
(Spinach or mushrooms can be used instead of salmon if you want.)

METHOD

Melt butter in a small saucepan and add the flour. Gently cook over low heat until mixture fully thickens.

Remove from heat and add yolks and sugar into the mix.

Beat egg whites until stiff but not dry and lumpy. Fold egg whites carefully into the mix.

Line a jelly roll tin with baking paper and pour in the mixture.

Cook in a pre heated 180°C oven for about 30 mins or until light brown.

When ready, place the roulade to cool slightly on a wire rack. While still warm, roll the roulade up into a tea towel and leave to cool completely.

Mix the cream cheese with the smoked salmon, sour cream and lemon zest.

When the roulade has cooled, spread the mixture over the roulade and re-roll.

At this point, the roulade can be stored in the fridge or frozen until needed.

To serve, you can either bake the chilled roulade or microwave it if it has been frozen.

If baking, the roulade needs to be at room temperature before it goes in the oven. Put it in glass baking dish, cover with foil and bake slowly in a moderate oven for about a half an hour. Cut into slices and serve with fresh smoked salmon and avocado.

To microwave, cut the slices while frozen. When roulade has thawed, wrap in glad wrap and put in microwave for about 30 seconds and serve.

Cheese fondue (similar to soufflé)

SERVES 4

INGREDIENTS

1 small minced onion
2 ozs butter
½ pint milk
1 cup fresh white breadcrumbs
2 eggs, separated
1 cup grated cheese
Pepper and salt

METHOD

Cook onion in butter until soft.

Add milk and pour over the breadcrumbs, the egg yolks and cheese.

Beat egg whites until firm. Fold in to the mixture.

Pour into buttered soufflé dishes.

Bake for ½ hour in a pre-heated 180°C oven.

THE INNER AND OUTER MATES

As my mother had created in her early years at Keayang, I too developed a special life away from the stressful situations that I encountered at Robe Terrace. The Inner and Outer Mates were first introduced to me in the late 1940s when there was a mass immigration of Western Europeans to Australia. My mother knew it was the right thing to employ those needing work, so the live-in staff, or Inner Mates, were all immigrants.

The first employed were a Ukrainian couple, Nadia and Ostarph. They did not speak English, so I helped them with it while my mother taught them how to cook and clean her way. They welcomed me into the kitchen and their lives. In their little back room, I learnt to speak Ukrainian and to dance the Ukrainian national dance, which I performed at the age of seven at the town hall at the United Nations Festival. I tasted yoghurt for the first time and mouth-watering yeast buns with prunes stuffed in their centres.

After Nadia and Ostarph left, two Greek girls, Sia and Despina, became part of the household. Despina stayed on for years and even moved in with my husband and me when we had our second child, Eliza. My mother taught Despina how to run the household exactly as she wanted. I learnt to speak Greek and she showed me how to make spanakopita and baklava. I had never heard of these Greek delicacies.

Then there were my Outer Mates. They were my friends who came regularly to the house: Pop the gardener and Widdy the washerwoman. Pop hung out in the garden shed – literally, 'it' all would have hung out if I had taken up his offer to touch his fly buttons. Widdy made huge bowls of blue starch for my father's shirts. The starch made his shirts so stiff they could stand up on their own. The other Outer Mates who came to our house were the tradies. The three that I remember best were the fishmonger, the bread man and the delivery boy. The fishmonger would come up the back garden path with fresh fish in

The United Nations Festival, 1949

one hand and a huge knife in stabbing mode in the other, with a very fierce look on his face. He was terrified of our dog, Samba, and thought she would attack him. She never did. He would fillet the fish in our kitchen and leave the same way he came in. The bread man had me to greet him at the back gate every morning. I would collect the still warm bread and, before I reached the house, I would eat the soft fat bit that stuck out once I had pulled the loaves apart. No one commented unless I went too far and dug a deep hole in the loaf, because then the first two slices were only crust! Later in the morning the Chinese fruit and vegetable man arrived in his old wooden cart with a high step up the back to a display of produce and the smell of ripe fruit. There I was again! Waiting at the door to be ushered up the steps to give the order and wait for my reward of a new-season apple.

My favourite Outer Mate owned the general store. I walked down to the shop almost every day with sixpence and came back with a huge bag of boiled sweets from the big glass jars on the top shelf. The owner would sometimes give me slices of 'fritz', cold sliced meat unique to South Australia, and out-of-date goodies for nothing. Eight years later I still went to visit the store, but this time on my bicycle. I went with the excuse to pick up orders for the kitchen, but I was really smitten by the errand boy, who was about ten years older than me. I rode around the neighbourhood in search of him doing errands, and made up excuses to visit the corner shop to catch a glimpse of him. He did not reciprocate my crush. I was just a little girl with her first unrequited love.

Such diverse characters sowed the seed that nourished and expanded my multicultural adventures and culinary skills for the rest of my life.

Last of all there were the chooks, my friends that lived at the bottom of the garden. I escaped there when I was in trouble, and I would sit on the perches with my chook mates, waiting for my parents to come and look for me. I hated it when Widdy cut the chooks' heads off and I would smell the feathers heating up in the pot.

My silent mates were the nuns and archbishop next door. I loved to peep through the slats in the fence and watch the nuns silently glide by the beautiful blue grotto that housed a statue of the Virgin Mary. Even better, the archbishop's bedroom was directly opposite my upstairs bedroom window where I used to observe him in the evenings, putting on his orange, blue and white striped flock pyjamas.

How did this loving, caring, sweet-natured seven-year-old grow up to become a completely dysfunctional emotional cripple by the age of sixteen?

EARLY YEARS

It is interesting to reflect on the role my parents played in those early years. My first view of my father every morning was through the shaving mirror in the bathroom. As I explained earlier, there was only one bathroom between the six of us. I was the first to be called at 7.00 am. As my bedroom was furthest away, my father could not hear me respond to his call, so for fifteen years I woke up to the sound of his bellowing voice and leapt out of bed. In order to avoid blacking out, I put my head on the side, so that my brain would think I was still lying down. Hence I was able to make the distance to where he could hear me say 'I'm coming'. This story is important because it set a pattern for instant and early rising for the rest of my life. The habit served me well in the hospitality business, as I always met my obligations in a professional kitchen. It seems unbelievable to think I could not ask my father for a different approach. Showering was an added trauma. I used to turn my nakedness to the wall so I could not see his piercing eyes watching me through the shaving mirror. I hated those looks and his intrusion.

I did not see my father in any other form until after work at 5.00 pm when I heard his key turn in the lock. My body would stiffen and my heart sink, as I felt cold fear in his presence. I spent a lot of time in the kitchen because it was the only safe place away from him. No wonder I learnt to cook. If I was called to the sitting room, it was to hold up his legs as he sat in his chair, or to allow him to yank my shoulders to get me to stand up straight, or to let him 'lift me to heaven' by my head. There were also his over the top 'jokes', like shaking and squeezing our wrapped gifts for him, which he often broke. Lastly, when guests invited me to play my piano accordion, he would send me down into the garden to play, where I could hardly be heard, and yell for me to go further away until I was finally down at the chook yard.

Dinner, at 6.45 pm every night, was the worst ordeal. My father was intoxicated by this point and at his worst, being critical, controlling and cruel. We had to put our hand up to get permission to speak and were made to recite elocution lessons, like 'how now brown cow?'. Sometimes he would use a broom to keep my shoulders back and shout at me to chew my food forty-four times, but worst of all was the continual barrage of interrogation and critical comments about anything I said. It seemed he enjoyed upsetting all of us, including my mother. All I ever wanted was for my mother to show love for me and for my father to disappear. I used to try to shrink his head as he sat opposite me at the dining room table. I got it to the size of a walnut and that's as far as it went. Often he would be left sitting alone at the table with his glass of wine as we had all left the table in tears.

Why did I never dare to question anything he did or said? Instead I internalised everything. The child, the scallywag, in me fought for life. I started writing poems, inspired by the sea at Kangaroo Island.

Suicide to the Sea

No sun, no moon, no one but me
To strain the sorrows of my heart,
Except communing with the sea
That one day would be part of me.

The sorrow in my heart was great,
All bitterness I had was gone,
As nothing here could make me hate
The sea that was to be my fate,
As time and life drew on.

And as the sun and heat of day
Had vanished from the eastern sky,
The surface of the sea lay dead,
Triumph resting on her bed
Where I was there to lie.

Then as the edge came nearer me
I knew that all I had would die,
As I closed my eyes to meet the sea
As she opened up her arms to me,
Stretched upwards to the sky.

Age: thirteen

My mother's home duties, staff training and creative endeavours definitely transported her away from the day-to-day struggles of dealing with my father's alcoholism throughout my adolescence. Grand dinners were at the top of her to-do list. My mother was conditioned to entertain. Of course, for these events there was a need for special costumes all made by my mother and her helper, Mrs Groom, who came to the house every week to sew. Initially, an Outer Mate would come to the front door with a suitcase full of fabric. My mother would purchase exotic cloth for eveningwear and children's clothes. Smocking and beading were her forte, and she later made all our wedding dresses. Jill and I were ungrateful for these homegrown models. We wanted shop-bought clothes that were out of my mother's control and choice. But those days I spent on the floor under my mother's feet making up clothes with scraps of fabric for my many dolls were the best days of my life at Robe Terrace, along with time spent in the kitchen with my Inner Mates. My antique dolls had real hair and bending wooden limbs and my animals, monkeys and bears all had a place in my bed every night. They protected me from the bombs, bogeymen, the dark, my father and the cold.

my best 'toy' friends!

I didn't see my mother much in the mornings; she stayed upstairs until we had gone to school. When we came home it was as if she had been upstairs all day, because we would call, 'Ma, I'm home,' bang down our school cases, and wait for the familiar 'Yeeees' to drift down the staircase. Of course she was around, attending to the staff's duties and her social responsibilities.

I had my friends in the kitchen so I didn't really care that Mum wasn't available. My main contact with her came after nursery tea and before lights out when she would come up for a ritual I have never forgotten, the one-minute prayer. During this time, my mother would sit on my bed with my arms around her neck reciting,

In my little bed I lie
Heavenly father hear my cry
Lord protect me through the night
And keep me safe till morning light
Amen

God bless Mother and Father, Mignon, Shylie and Jill
and all the sick soldiers, and all my poor cousins,
and make me a good girl
For Christ's sake
Amen

THE UPPER CRUST

After the Depression and war, there was a resurgence of optimism and excitement about new beginnings. My mother started the ball rolling by putting on charity dinners and balls to raise money for organisations like the Red Cross. There were not as many choices of food available as there are today, but my mother oversaw the production of simple, fresh, beautifully prepared meals with style.

The grand dinners were a huge production. On the morning of the event, the flowers arrived, picked by one of my mother's secret admirers from his gardens. Outer Mates then arrived to set up for the evening. The table (sometimes there were four) in the ballroom was beautifully set with flowers, crystal and silver. My mother would direct the food preparation for the whole morning. Later in the afternoon, Widdy the washerwoman usually put too much starch in father's stiff-fronted shirts with their mother-of-pearl studs. Sometimes he could not bend. He would sweat profusely, mop himself and slather on his unpleasant smelling aftershave, then take a huge sniff of his benzedrine inhaler that he carried with him at all times (addicted, I'm sure). Then he proceeded down to the bar to prepare cocktails.

As soon as my mother had everything under control, I would sit up in her dressing room and watch while she was 'putting on her face', as she liked to call it. I always thought she looked beautiful with her auburn hair and simple elegance. The Inner Mates would also change into pale grey uniforms with little organza caps, cuffs and aprons trimmed with lace. Then we were all ready for the upper crust to arrive. Cocktails were in the living-cum-bar room. The bar was the hub of the house. Built into the wall, it was like a small room, displaying about thirty bottles of liqueur and spirits. My father's position was behind the bar from the moment the guests arrived and for the next hour and a half. Then George the butler moved everyone into the ballroom for dinner.

The best experience for me came next. When the leftovers of delicious food came out of the door, I got to pounce on them. I would always be at the door waiting for the buzzer, which my mother had set up near her foot under the carpet. She pressed it for staff to serve and clear away. Staff had their share too, and they were often quite tipsy by the end of the night. They didn't think I could see their half-finished glasses hiding in corners of the kitchen, not that I could have cared less. By now I was all for supporting the underdogs, or the Inner Mates.

If there happened to be a three-piece band and dancing, I would remove myself to my next position, peering through the crack in the ballroom door while they glided around the dance floor. I loved the live music and the beautiful clothes. Many hours later when I'd gone to my room, I was able to eavesdrop on the gossip from all the ladies who would retire to the bathroom to powder their noses. When all the noise had died down at about two in the morning, I was awakened by my father's footsteps on the stairs, as he came up with a huge jug of tomato juice, Worcester sauce, ice and celery sticks, which he would munch just outside my door. The hangover cure was about to commence.

There were very few restaurants in those days, and certainly none with liquor licences, so entertaining at home suited my father, too, for both private affairs and business dinners. Anyway, he loved my mother's cooking so much that restaurants were never an option for the rest of his life.

I also loved my mother's cooking, and anything I occasionally didn't like I would hide in the garden or flush down the lavatory because you could never leave anything on your plate. I couldn't bear to waste food, so in the early dining-out days at other people's homes or hotels, I would hide it in my bag until I got home. When the first large hotel opened in Adelaide I went to the opening, and when we were given a complimentary Peach Melba as an extra dessert I loaded it into my mother's hand-sewn beaded bag that she had loaned me, just managing to close the clasp over the cream. Of course, I forgot about it when I got home. The bag went back into her cupboard, only to be found moulding away when my mother next wanted to use it!

My first cooking experience with my mother was rolling out homemade pastry with dirty hands (which made it grey) into tart shapes and filling them with jam. After that, I made beautiful lunches to take to school. I couldn't wait to eat them to calm my school anxieties, so I ate them for recess and came home for lunch, as we lived just around the corner.

Sunday was the only day we girls had sole use of the kitchen, as it was the staff's day off. As long as we cleaned up afterwards, we could do what we wanted. Usually our experiments were based around toffee, fudge and biscuits.

My first paid catering job was at the age of ten. I wanted to buy myself a piano accordion, and I came up with a moneymaking idea of offering breakfast in bed to the family. I charged them sixpence (five cents) each. I would serve sardines in fried bread, sausages chopped up in white sauce or tins of baked beans from the pantry. My parents told me the truth about my strange menu, but when guests came to stay, they were too nice to complain and suffered in silence, and I got my piano accordion after six months.

PENIS ENVY

The problem was we were all girls. We tried being boys. We knew our father was desperate to have one. We tried changing our names. I became Robert and Mignon became Colin. Jill and I played cowboys and Indians for hours and one Christmas Day cut out moustaches and wore them all day.

In my teens, I was a hot shot with a .44 and liked going shooting or to Rowley Park Speedway with my mates. I did not take offence when I was occasionally told, 'Shut up, Belinda, or I'll set light to the wick of your tampax and blow your box to bits!!'

It took me a long time to establish balance in my sexuality. The feminine side did not really find a place until after my divorce. I had never seen my parents naked and I had no idea how boys were constructed. My first experience of the male appendage was at the age of seven.

I was walking back from the shop one afternoon and there was a young man astride his motorbike outside our house. As I passed he said, 'Hello, little girl. Come over here and touch this.' I always did what I was told so I sauntered over and what I saw seemed very unusual. Out of a hole in his leather pants protruded a greyish white slug. Obediently, I touched it and walked off.

My next experience was even stranger. It happened while on holidays with my sisters and cousins at Keayang. As I wandered alone in the extensive outdoor area we called 'the Magic Garden', one of my cousins popped out from behind a bush and said, 'Okay. I suppose you'd better come in. We're playing doctors and hospitals.' I crawled into the bushes to be confronted by Leonard, the fourteen-year-old gardener's son, coming from the so-called hospital with a huge purple cabbage leaf wrapped around the same slug I had seen before. This looked shocking and angry, surrounded by the colour and texture of the leaf. I ran off in fright.

Later in my life I had enormous respect for the male genitalia, when it was presented in its proper perspective. I had no sexual explanation or information from my mother. I did not understand that the rubber balloons I found in the gutter and the ones my sister filled with water and stuck on her handlebars were condoms. I thought the man standing on the box behind the horse in the park across the road didn't know how to ride. What was I to make of the words my father used as an endearment to my mother, like, 'silly old twat'? What hope did I have for a positive entree to my own sexuality? None. I was afraid of sex, pregnancy and bad reputation without much explanation from my parents. All I knew was that I was definitely a virgin when I got married.

In my twenties I heard about another penis experience, which happened at my mother's closest friend's house. They were seriously upper crust people. A party was put on for a very famous prima ballerina and her Russian partner. As they were sitting on the couch with their Adelaide director, he presented them, at eye level, with a huge hors d'oeuvres platter resplendent with olives, cheeses and prosciutto. Tucked in cleverly between his crutch and the plate was what looked like a chorizo sausage, but it definitely was not!

Dick for a Day

I'd love a dick for a day
And pass the time away – pulling it!
Then hope that it would fit
Into some cosy hole (no loathsome moll)
A virgin would be best,
Then after a short rest,
I'd take on a whole team
Of winsome girls,
Oh! What a dream
I'd make them scream (with joy)
My lovely toy,
With whom I'd like to play
My dick for a day.

Age: thirty-five

LOST AND LONELY IN THE WILDERNESS

The start of my school years could have been a reprieve from home life . . . but it wasn't. The private school I attended just around the corner had the appearance of desolation the minute I walked through the gates. It was called Wilderness, and I was lost and lonely in its wilderness of asphalt, dust, olive trees and high fences that closed us off from the outside world. It is very different now, but at that time it could have been Auschwitz! Brown uniforms, brown environment, military-type discipline. It was all so proper. The shell of my existence was perfectly shaped and coloured to match my environment. But inside were so many contradictions, and ideas that did not match.

I very soon learned how to lie, cheat, and avoid homework and sport. My undetected dyslexia attracted condemnation from teachers and ridicule from students. I failed all exams and survived only by becoming the practical joker: a rebel with a cause, the clown in the class. Laughed at, not with. Fearful of evenings at home dealing with my dad and dreading school, I tried to stay awake late into the night, only to disappear like a lump of shit into the arsehole of the earth every morning.

But there were two achievements I took some pride in. Firstly, there was my distinction in art, and, secondly, my ability to write back-to-front, which I did as quickly as normal forward writing.

I still enjoy both.

KANGAROO ISLAND . . . IN THE BEGINNING

As a family we spent all our school holidays on Kangaroo Island, off the coast of South Australia. In those days it took a whole day by boat to get there from Port Adelaide, and then four hours by car, which included various stops for supplies, and brandy and ice drinks for the adults. From 1942 (the year I was born), I never missed a trip until adulthood. My father shipped over an old shack, reconstructing it on the sandhills at Snelling Beach, and paid rent to the farmer of one pound a year. It was primitive – no power, gaslights, a wood stove and hand-pumped water. We bought large ice blocks from Kingscote, which were kept in a large wooden chest to cool food in. Away in the sandhills there were two long-drop lavatories, one for men and one for women. The shower was called an APC – armpits and crutch. It was a bucket with holes in it to pull up for showering under, which lasted less than a minute.

Early mornings started by being awakened by Pop the gardener, who came with us from Adelaide, delivering hot tea and toast he'd cooked on the wood stove. My father insisted on segregation of sleeping arrangements, so 'females', as he called us, slept in one bedroom, and the men slept in the other. After toast my father presented himself in his sarong, with brandy and milk for the adults. 'One glass to get the left wing off the ground, the second for the right wing.' My mother hid her drinks in her bedside table cupboard rather than reject my father's offering.

At eight o'clock, my mother would take over the kitchen for the unbelievable breakfast procedure. Every morning my father insisted on battered whiting that he had caught in his boat the day before. The wood stove had to be stoked very hot to get the oil to the right temperature. By the time she had cooked about sixteen pieces, her face was the same colour as the lobster we ate for lunch, but the praise for her batter was enough for her to keep it up for the next twenty years.

It was a very different life on the island for my mother. Many years later, she admitted that deep down she really didn't enjoy it, although I think it was a good balance for all of us from all the palaver at Robe Terrace.

While on the island, we had a different kind of contact with my father. We learnt from his discipline and work ethic, both of which became essential in my future. Chop the wood, cart the wood, pump the water, fillet the fish, dig out the lavatories, meet the boat when the fishermen came home and then clean the boat. I loved island life in every way. It created a weird type of freedom within this strange family. I saw Dad in a different way. Although he still controlled everything, there was a lighter edge to him. Afternoons were free and it was

Belinda as Robert, 1949

only a gong ringing out in the sand dunes that would bring me home.

Every day, weather permitting, there were morning fishing trips, accompanied by one bottle of brandy, water and two blocks of dark chocolate. After meeting the boat and cleaning the fish, it was drinking time again. Then a huge lunch of crayfish that was kept alive in a rock pool and cooked on the wood stove, which had to be kept going all day. In the summer heat, this was unbearable in a tin and fibro shack. After lunch, siestas were compulsory, and then we had afternoon tea of fresh scones, jam and tea. Soon five o'clock came and it was drinks on the verandah. At seven, another banquet of roasted and boiled meats, soups and old-fashioned puddings. Lastly we children had to do the washing up in a tin bowl with a kettle full of boiling water.

Reflecting on this time, the most distinctive difference between Robe Terrace and Kangaroo Island was the integration of our family, which I loved. No dining room dramas and a freedom to be, instead of do. This must have been how Dad felt as well, because he was happier on Kangaroo Island, and his happier mood affected us all.

CAST OUT OF SCHOOL

At fourteen my introverted, protected world fell apart when I was forced to go to a doctor after being plagued with an aching leg for over six months. I could not believe it when I was told I would have to wear a plaster cast from my neck down to my hips to straighten a crooked spine. I refused to go back to school, or to see anyone. My waist was 31 inches and my tits, which were just beginning to grow, were squashed like two pancakes against my chest. Two months stretched into nine, and by this time I felt as if the stinking plaster, which they never changed, was with me forever. Each time I took a deep breath, the putrid smell of unwashed flesh flooded my nostrils. It was such a destructive time; I lacked any sense of direction or self-worth. When finally the plaster came off, I was dismayed to find I could not even bend over. My spine was like jelly and I had absolutely no shape. The monotonous procedure of going to the physiotherapist twice a week started before I was able to move again. Things went from bad to worse. I felt awkward, being nearly five foot nine inches tall and spotty with knocked knees. Feeling very sorry for myself, encouragement from my mother did nothing for my disposition. I wrote sad songs, drew sad pictures and spent most of my time at home.

On returning to school, I failed my public exams twice and in desperation my parents let me leave school to learn shorthand and typing. Most days, however, I did not even get to college, but would hop off the bus and sit in the park until it was time to go home.

After a month, I left shorthand and typing classes altogether. Instead, I learned guitar, did a course in fashion design, and another in photographic modelling. I joined a theatre company and learned to cook from my mother. It did not take me long to realise I needed a purpose to my life. It was time to get a job to pay for my creative adventures. But what could I do with no qualifications and no formal training? I had always loved children, so when a position came up as aide to the schoolteachers at a local 'spastic' home, I took it.

I will never forget the first day – I presented myself in white uniform and shoes to the superintendent, who explained my duties. On arrival of the buses, I was to take all the children to the lavatory and collect the resident children from 'the other side'. One by one they were lined up in their wheelchairs along the wall, awaiting my assistance. They were heavy and awkward, some in full calipers and body braces, their legs to be secured in specially made slots in their seats. They misfired to the floor, and flooded their pants. Diarrhea in calipers meant I had to remove it with a paintbrush. There was vomit on the floor that would not wipe up with a squeegee mop. It was hard to cope with the dry retching and the horror of physical and visual trauma all around me.

Once this job was complete, I made my way to the 'other side', down the corridor and into a room marked 'recreation', with a sickly sweet smell mixed with disinfectant. Around the room were a couple of dozen inmates ranging between four and forty, all in different stages of oral and manual gratification – chewing and regurgitating food, screaming or trying to find a hole in their clothes that had been securely sewn up. I grabbed the necessary children and fled back down the passage only to be met by a very well developed nineteen-year-old male with not a stitch on. He had escaped from a nurse while she was trying to change his nappy. He proceeded to gallop after me, back to the schoolroom where I burst in to take refuge behind the teacher. At this moment, the little boy I was wheeling peed in a huge arc across the schoolroom, which landed with a splatter on a little boy's desk.

I could not believe my duties. I didn't feel I had the perseverance to go on, but I did, and I often wondered what it was that kept me there, considering my past lack of drive. After one year as teacher's aide, bus driver and on meal duties, they saw my potential for occupational therapy and I was transferred and fully trained as an aid to the physiotherapist. I learnt the difference between 'spastic', athetoid, 'Mongol' (Down syndrome) and haemophilia and I was given groups for classes in art and music. On weekends, I even took home some children who had no visits from their parents. This was where my parents showed kindness to the 'poor people'. I grew to love those children. They were so grateful and accepting, and the ones with severe retardation had such special qualities to compensate. For the first time in my life I really felt worthwhile. I felt I could learn and accept difficult responsibilities. This was a turning point toward hope in my future.

OUTRAGEOUS BEHAVIOUR

The boyfriends, the stylish dinners, secretiveness and outrageous behaviour. How did it all begin? It probably started one weekend during the nine-month period of the plaster cast. My mother and I were invited to an enormous station up north for a weekend with a family I had always looked upon as rich and stuffy. I did not want to go, but my mother insisted, and that was her mistake.

Me with my .22, 1960

Lady Mawson-Smith had a son about my age who had invited his girlfriend for the weekend. In addition there were other members of the family all in residence. The madness started at dinner that night when all were seated at a long refectory table. Lady Mawson-Smith's son Tim was at one end of the table and I was at the other. As if by telepathy we both lifted the table off the floor at the same moment. Manoeuvring with our knees, we managed to shoot it away, just as Lady Mawson-Smith was about to put her spoon in her soup. The look of horror on her and my mother's face, I have never forgotten. Undaunted we proceeded to keep the table rotating so that everyone was struggling desperately to retain their food, or grab it as it came past. Tim and I were nearly doubled over with laughter. As soon as dinner was finished we escaped, leaving the girlfriend behind. We then got some dead rabbits from traps, which we put into beds around the house, and then short-sheeted his mother's bed. Next we found a firefighting pump and squirted water all over the house. This only stopped when my mother dragged me off to bed. She was speechless with rage and humiliation.

A whack followed, but it hurt her more than me. She'd forgotten about the plaster cast!

Tim went back to school interstate after that weekend of fun, but his correspondence was incessant, funny, with interesting letters that put colour in my life, and I began to feel I was 'in love' for the first time. I built up the idea of a wonderful reunion. I longed for my first kiss. In the interim, my thick smelly plaster came off, and was replaced by a polyurethane one with an opening down the front so I could have a shower. The day of Tim's return came and we planned to go out together that night. Where we went early evening I can't recall, but I remember with great clarity the end of the evening, and the end of him. We parked in a quiet section of the gardens and sat talking, but when I stopped all I could hear were the laces of the polyurethane corset rubbing and squeaking with every breath. I tried to shallow breathe, hold my breath, and when he eventually turned to kiss me, I was stiff with fear. With my mouth taken care of, the creaking got worse and I was unaware of any sensation of pleasure. It was the one and only kiss that passed between my first love and me. I never saw him again.

VIRGINITY ON A PLATE

From that moment on, I truly believed all I was worth in this difficult world was to be laughed at. So I quickly developed my sense of the ridiculous, and wore glossy, flashy outfits over my wounded pride. When a lovely country boy came into my life, sensitive and wanting to encourage the real me, I was so convinced I was not really what he wanted I stepped over him and on to bigger and brighter things.

And then Jeremy came into my life. He would come around to my friend Lisa's house prepared for any sort of madness. Bottle after bottle of champagne was consumed. We would fall into fits of laughter under the table, with heads spinning; we were provocative, fearless and free of restrictions. Speeding cars, running through parks late at night, lost clothing, finally falling into bed – in separate beds at Lisa's house, which

My true image of myself, and the image I displayed for the outside world

became my second home – with a boy who had the worst reputation in town and who had no idea or care for social graces. When the games were over, I felt real feelings of warmth and togetherness and pleasure with Jeremy, which is what I remember most. How could tenderness accompany so much wildness? How did I keep my virginity, which I pretended to be handing out on a silver plate?

I had no shame and no remorse for my secret life. The hangovers (and there were plenty) were pleasant reminders of the night before, and felt so sinful and secretive that they were really a delicious experience. The more I felt it, the more I wanted it. And I remember struggling with the secrets I had to put away, to prepare me for another demanding day at the spastic centre.

On a personal level, at seventeen my image and personality were nowhere near the Griselda I had created in my imagination. Shape had not come back to my body properly. After the plaster came off, my skin was spotty, I felt too tall, and I lacked a clear identity, so I started painting my idea of a perfect expression on my own personal canvas: my face. Dark mascara, black dye to change rather mousy hair, heavy pancake makeup, accentuated lips and tits, and lots of exposure of my now quite shapely legs. With the outward change in looks came an extroverted personality. Nothing was too outrageous. The songs I wrote were bawdy and suggestive. The things I did were crazy and funny, and everything I said provocative. I was purging myself of a miserable self-image. Away from my parents' eyes, I was the cockteaser, the siren dressed to attract, only to reject at the final moment of surrender. Underlying all of that, I had a deep sense of morals and a terrifying fear of pregnancy.

Who was this girl who wore her appropriate little outfits, passed around the cocktail savouries and made polite noises after being summoned unwillingly from her upstairs room? The same person who cleaned up sick! And where did she go after dark, away from her parents' eagle eyes? I went to Lisa's house, around the corner. Her parents were simple folk and left her alone on the weekends, and it was there I acted out my fantasies. At seventeen, Belinda, the social butterfly from a very respectable family, could behave like a sinful woman/child. The purchase of oysters and champagne and hours of preparation in an empty house set the stage to play at being grown-up. Lisa and I spent many days at the first gelato bar in Adelaide, which had opened up in Hindley Street, and we both fell in love at the same time, so our daytime weekend antics continued into the evenings. We planned our adventures – intimate dinners for four, large picnics for forty, fast cars and booze, and lots of laughs. On the rare occasions when my parents were away, we set up the ballroom for a unique extravaganza – Elizabethan, Roman or Bollywood feasts. One particular night, five of us decided to sleep in my parents' huge king-sized bed. We put on my dad's silk pajamas and all slipped between the silk sheets. There was no suggestion of sex, but simply three girls and two boys enjoying a lot of laughter and having fun!

Next morning when everyone had left, Lisa would help me tidy up, re-iron the sheets, and clean everything within an inch of its lives, before my parents got home Sunday night. Anyone looking on would think 'provocative, decadence; unruly teenagers with no morals or respect for their elders'. Morals we had, but we absolutely didn't have respect for the lavish lifestyles we lived at home.

Cooking had given my creativity wings to fly. I could produce my own dinner parties with enormous amounts of effort and care for detail. It made me feel confident, secure and gave me a purpose in life, and it allowed others to experience something that was truly memorable. Where did the inspiration and intricate concepts come from? Maybe they came from my ethnic Inner Mates, maybe genetics, or past life experiences. They could hardly have been gleaned from watching my parents' parties through a crack in the door! Their shows were all about formality – English aristocracy and polished silver. Most of my cooking skills were learned when my mother was teaching our live-in staff at Robe Terrace.

So with use of the family car, an allowance spent on food, and a place for entertaining – the top room – I could bring my unusual friends home, away from my parents' scrutiny. I would raid the cellar under the house for wine, and I could do what I liked behind that closed door.

WELCOME TO 'LA LA' AND 'WOO WOO' LAND

'La la' land could be explained as an expression of my social life at Robe Terrace, but it was so much more. It was about unrealistic expectations, a fantasy world, out of control behaviour, inevitable repercussions, instability and chaos, all nestled around (thank goodness) a certain sense of a work ethic, that seemed the only stability keeping me grounded and financially secure.

Then the other far more obscure aspect of 'la la' land was a combination of creativity with a sense of humour, ridiculousness and a clown syndrome, so often exposed in dysfunctional but creative people. I didn't understood until much later that this behavior in the right context was a blessing. I went through so much – introspection, reflection and forgiving of myself – before I could see the true worth of creative outlets.

My mental health issues resulting from too much 'la la' land led me to to 'woo woo' land, a spiritually ignited journey into metaphysics and clairvoyance. My first encounter with metaphysics was as early as ten years old. My mother was fascinated with gypsies coming to the house and reading tea leaves. With my insistent pestering, she agreed I could have a turn, and I will never forget what the gypsy lady told me: I would have four children. As my only dream at this time was to leave home, get married and have babies, I was exhilarated.

Not really understanding her methods of revelation, I put it all aside until a year and a half after I was married and had not become pregnant. In my fear, I remembered what she said and put hope in her words. What is extraordinary even today is that I did eventually have four pregnancies – Nick, Eliza, Rachel, and an abortion at four months after a botched tubal ligation.

BANDSTAND

In among my culinary and romantic adventures, I had begun to compile a repertoire of compositions with guitar. Although my voice was not exceptional, the songs were. Nothing quite like them had been written before. For example, one was called 'Deep Freeze', which was all about freezing your man so that you could thaw him out when you needed him. I sang my compositions to my friends and they seemed to like them. It was not until a visit to Sydney that things really started to move.

I was playing at a party when a chap approached me and asked me if I would like to go on television. I thought it was a joke. He said he was the cameraman for a national pop show, Brian Henderson's *Bandstand*. Not really believing it was possible, I accepted his invitation to meet the directors. I chose 'Deep Freeze' and followed it with 'You're Going to Miss Me When I'm Gone'. I sat up on the boardroom table and sang away without a care in the world. When it was all over, I could hardly believe that they invited me on to the show. I don't know how I did it!

A nineteen-year-old, untrained guitar-plucking nobody, thrown into a studio with a full orchestra and no audience, just the huge red eye of the camera staring back at me. The show was taped, which made me feel better, and there was a rehearsal in the afternoon to warm up.

Bandstand, 1961

They asked for my score. What score? They asked what key best suited my voice. What key? I did not have a clue and they were fascinated. After rehearsals I had to present myself for makeup and hair, and I came face-to-face with the pop idols of the day – Col Joye, Patsy Ann Noble, Normie Rowe, the Delltones. This was when the excitement started for me. I came out with a new face and new hair, wearing a cream lace dress with a plunging neckline and spike-heel shoes.

The actual performance was a blur. 'You're on now, Belinda. Sing to the camera with the light and relax. Smile, and good luck.' Seven minutes and it was all over. There was applause and whistles away from the hot lights. I was so proud of myself and couldn't believe I had got through without a slip. Next day's paper said some nice things. Returning to Adelaide the door was open wide to the television world, and I stepped in.

Offers came from every station. I had supposedly cracked the big time. I was invited to receptions to meet the Beatles at the town hall when they came to Adelaide in the 1960s, and Tom Jones in Sydney the same year. Television extended to cabaret and I needed more songs and more practice, and I still had a job and crazy boyfriend, Jeremy, to cope with. With all this publicity I began feeling the strain of personal expectations and the superficiality of the medium and pressure. I came out in a rash just prior to a performance. I was worried I was not good enough. What used to be a pleasure now became agony, but I decided the agony must go on. I pushed myself into more and more performances: cabaret, theatre, television, commercials and modelling. Deep breathing and a swig of brandy always helped to relax my nerves.

At the end of my second trip to Sydney, to appear on *The Dave Allen Show*, I encountered Mr Sin. Lee Gordon was Australia's top talent promoter both locally and internationally, and Mr Sin was his talent scout. Mr Sin came around to where I was staying in Sydney after he heard me sing. I was excited at the prospect of meeting the infamous

Publicity shot, 1961

Glamour, 1962

Lee. I had visions of becoming a big movie star – but it did not turn out quite like that. Mr Sin was to take me to meet Lee.

'There is more to meeting Lee Gordon than just being a good singer,' he said. 'He is very selective and fussy, and a bit kinky about his promoting of talent – it has to encompass everything. He sleeps in a coffin, you know.'

I looked at him in utter amazement.

'What are you into?' he asked, his beady eyes boring into me.

I didn't know what to answer; I felt foolish and dumb.

'Listen,' he said, 'I can train you how to be Lee Gordon's girlfriend. I know exactly what he likes and wants. It's the only way to ensure you will get the right attention.'

He moved over and put his hands on the top of my legs. I froze, then turned and ran out of the room and around the corner out of sight, where I stood getting my thoughts together. Was it possible that there were people in the world like this, willing to abuse and exploit people for their own ends? Was this the only way to reach the top? I wondered how many people got where they wanted on their own initiative. How could one have any pride after being subjected to such sick values? Then I took a look at myself – dressed to provoke, an aura of sexuality, hair piled up like Brigitte Bardot, skirt above my knees, heavy makeup, pouting lips, with a handful of suggestive songs. No wonder he thought I was good material. 'What a phony,' I thought. 'I might look like a sex symbol, but I am not prepared to accept this.' Going back to the house, I made sure he was gone, and burst into tears.

I felt too much pressure on *The Dave Allen Show.* This was really Big Time. I was in a segment for best new talent with original compositions. I'd written a song especially for the show about – would you believe – Beatle mania. But it was really about my disposition. It felt like the end of an era and it was. I went back to Adelaide and dyed my hair bright scarlet, took off half the face paint, and put away my songbook.

THE FOURSOME

Back in Adelaide, the Lisa and Jeremy connection continued. I knew that my parents would totally disapprove of Jeremy. He was rough and uncouth, so having a hideaway at Lisa's house was essential. She didn't mind that I climbed in her window in the middle of the night, and her parents didn't mind that I parked my car in their space or that I was loud and bossy. They trusted me implicitly. Lisa was my ally; she was a constant source of fun and acceptance. Our pranks were pretty harmless, and how lucky were we, having boyfriends who we could spend whole nights with without them actually 'putting it in'!

As a foursome – she with her boyfriend 'Scarface', and me with Jeremy – we had the most terrific time. There was no pretence or bullshit. Deep down there was a desperate need for us to fill our emotional gaps and feelings of worthlessness. If we had not been able to laugh, we would have cried. Jeremy was in the worst emotional state. At nineteen he was well on the way to becoming an alcoholic. When he had a few too many drinks he became aggressive and impossible. It was this side of him that caused our eventual demise. My drinking habits were different. I would begin the night with a few strong brandies to light my wick and I could then burn brightly all night.

My parents were anxious to know where I was and what I was doing, but I expect it was a relief for them to see I was busy and happier than in the past. They were right to trust my morals, but wrong to trust my honesty. It was not unusual for me to lie my way through great chunks of the week, and it didn't really bother me. I felt I had to protect my choices and direction. There was something very gutsy about the rough edges of the crowd I spent all my time with. There were no hidden meanings or feelings – a look of lust was very obvious, a punch in the nose equally unequivocal. Under the tough exteriors there was a lot of genuine warmth. In their company I always felt wanted and very much female.

In this period of my life the top room took on a different atmosphere. Gone were the books and navy blue walls of my sisters' era. Everyone had got married and it was now my room. And how flashy it was, with gold walls, polished floorboards, a huge white rug, a little bar, comfortable chairs and amber dim lights. Creativity did not end in this area. The walls of my bedroom were an eye opener, with murals of tough-looking boys in leather and ripple-soled shoes, a purple plant, a half-human creature and, across the mantelpiece, the current boyfriend's car. When one boyfriend was superseded, I would paint the new car in front of the old (there were only half a dozen up there all told).

EUROPE

While Lisa's relationship was flourishing, Jeremy's heavy bouts of drinking and bad behaviour were starting to get me down, so a proposed trip to stay with my aunt in the English countryside, 'to finish me off', came at a very good time. I said farewell to Jeremy from Melbourne. I was travelling on an inexpensive Italian ship via the Panama. My cabin was crazy. I was on a deck below the waterline and above the hot oil tanks, which meant I needed my shoes on to get out of bed. It was a little black room with two bunks and just enough room for a washbasin and cupboard. This would be my home for the next five weeks.

Baggage stowed, and full of seasick pills, I made my way up what seemed a hundred miles to air and light and to the roughest seas I had ever seen. The decks and main function rooms were deserted. It was almost impossible to stand up. Everyone was ill and I am sure my salvation was my father's advice to take the pills before departure. Suddenly I felt very lonely. Gone were my family, Lisa and Jeremy. Not only were my surroundings strange, but I was surrounded by the ocean with no way to get off.

Everyone appeared the following night for dinner. There were set seating arrangements and one quick look was enough to confirm the dreary selection at my table – Mrs Mouse and her new spouse, and two elderly ladies. I was about to make my escape when up came the last person to join our table. She was a young, very attractive English girl who introduced herself as Janet. She had come to Australia to marry an Australian boy, and on this same ship had fallen in love with the ship's doctor, a suave and handsome Italian. She then cancelled the wedding and booked herself back on the same ship, to carry on the affair.

We immediately clicked. She was great company on what would have been a very long and boring trip. Having travelled on this ship before, she knew all the ropes, so after dinner on that first night we went to the bar for a drink and Janet pointed out her Italian lover. We sat for a while and watched the charade – girls by the dozen, like a field of wildflowers, filled the bar, overshadowing the few beer-swilling 'ocker' males. Lounging against the bar and strutting about were the 'others' – the crisp whiteness of uniform, deep tan and good looks of the Italian officers. One hundred wildflowers were waiting to be plucked by a dozen or so men. Amazing! An officer would make his choice and invite a girl to the bar for a drink. If she fitted the requirements he would ask her to a late night party in his cabin (for two) and that was how Janet had met Roberto. While I sat hiding in the corner, Janet wandered over to Roberto. 'There goes my friend for the rest of the trip,' I thought. But no, back she came. Roberto was on duty until late and wouldn't be free. He was not free for her for the rest of the voyage. Poor Janet: her anguish, her shattered dreams, and, what was worse, she thought she was pregnant. If I had not had her to think about and help through a difficult time, I would have gone mad. I could not help being amused as the wild flowers became very limp and disillusioned and one by one they were cast aside. Expectations turned to disappointment after a one-night stand. My mother had warned me about not mixing martinis with sailors. But as the officers with their arrogance were by far the most interesting males on board, I was tempted into stage one – at the bar, with each one of them – but never accepted stage two.

Showing off on board, 1961

Janet and I in Venice, 1961

As the trip continued Janet and I spent more time on our own. We slept till lunch, and joined in all the shipboard fun of 'crossing the line', fancy dress, and I even sang a few songs with the band. The ports of call were the best part: Tahiti, Jamaica and Portugal – the colour, noise and foreign languages, all so exciting. The contrast to Australia made me realise what a small and sheltered chunk of life I had been living. On my last night I sang a song I composed, directed at the officers and the girls on board.

Beware everyone of this trip you've begun
For what romance will capture you here,
Beware of that guy with a look in his eye
It's a look you should learn how to fear.
The girls I must warn, of a white uniform
And a manner that leads you astray,
Although love he'll declare, it's not long you'll be there,
He is just out for some easy prey.
A ship is a life that will lead you to strife,
For a whim and a fancy you'll fall,
With the hot tropic air, it's a hard strain to bear,
But I bet you won't bear it at all.
They don't love you it's true, any girl's good as you,
Don't be led to believe what they say,
They will ask you for one drink, Ah that's what you think.
They are just out for some easy prey.

Age: nineteen

My nine months abroad were not a huge success, mainly because I was not a huge success, or even a little success. Sawbridgeworth in Hertfordshire was a beautiful country town and in years to come I would find my Aunt Lorie a lot of fun, but I did not appreciate that side of her when I was still only nineteen. I was so caught up with my own

Performing on board the *Fairstar*, 1961

image and impact that I did not really listen to her. I was supposed to be clever and witty and beautiful, but in the eyes of most people I met, I was none of these things. To them I was loud, flashy and not the image of aristocracy. In return, I found English girls wishy-washy and English men stuffy. I was extremely homesick, cold and lacking in spirit, and with my aunt there seemed no escape, just good sensible living!

As the weeks dragged on and I had eaten the corner shop out of cakes and put on nearly a stone, I decided to move to London. I got a room in a flat in Chelsea, owned by a friend of my mother's. It was a five-storey terrace house and I shared the top flat with an Englishman. I only saw him three times on the stairs, but smelt him often since he only took a bath once a week. My days were spent walking and bussing around London. The highlight of this time for me was when a publishing company took two of my songs and I managed an audition with the BBC. It never eventuated into anything more. A bout of tonsillitis put me in hospital to have my tonsils removed and it was not a pleasant operation. I was so ill afterwards that Lorie took me back to Sawbridgeworth to recover. I became even more miserable until plans were made to send me to Italy to the warm weather. My sister Jill had an old friend, a signora who hosted boarders in Florence.

With low spirits I boarded the plane to Italy, wishing it was the plane home – I'd had enough. I moved from the extreme cold of London, to the warm air of Italy, where the atmosphere felt electric. Everyone seemed so excited. About what? I could not understand a word of Italian, but had my address written down to give to the taxi driver. Borgo Pinti was almost in the centre of Florence, near the huge mosaic Duomo, the landmark of the city. I was given a lovely big room with wooden floors and inlaid wooden furniture and a balcony looking out over the narrow street. Signora Patritzi, a woman of about eighty who could speak reasonable English, suggested I go to Italian lessons, which I took up and attended every morning.

I hated it. Any structured learning – teachers and students and homework – reminded me of school. I lasted about two weeks, but while I didn't enjoy the study, I found everything about Italy wonderful. It was exciting just to step into the street with people laughing and shouting and enjoying themselves. Florence was beautiful. I never got sick of walking down the old cobbled stone paths, exploring the shops on the Ponte Vecchio or taking a bus to nearby towns. The attention from the male population was astounding, too – whatever made me look so good to the locals here, when I was so unappealing to the English? Being quite tall, I stood out in the crowd, and also not knowing the traditions of the country, my wardrobe was quite disastrous. Low necklines and short skirts were very out of place, and sent the Italians into a frenzy. The men would follow me everywhere, even running me off the footpath with their Lambrettas. Police would stop on traffic duty to yell out 'Bella!' A boy ran his bicycle into a stationary car while taking a look at me. At first I loved it, then it got to be a bit of a nuisance, so I went to an Italian dressmaker and had her make me up some more respectable clothes to blend in. Meanwhile my Italian improved, not because of the lessons but because I had to speak it to get around. In those days there were not as many tourists and very few Florentines spoke English. Although I had company only at mealtimes, I was never bored, unhappy or lonely, and I even had a touch of romance.

Signora Patrizi introduced me to three Italian Air Force boys and we all went out for coffee and listened to music. When we got to Piazza Michelangelo, they decided three was a crowd, so I was expected to choose one. I did not have the courage to say which one, so I said – in my

A cheeky photo bomber, 1961

broken Italian – that I'd dance with each of them and the best dancer was the winner. I knew whom I wanted anyway. What eventuated was my almost silent friendship with Alberto. He was tall and fair and very good-looking and we spent the next week before my departure walking, dancing and kissing all over Florence. He carried with him a perpetual erection. It was frustrating for both of us. I'm sure he would have been a very nice boy if I'd been able to speak to him properly. I was sad to leave Italy, but I had to go back to my Aunt Lorie. Italy had given me new hope and an air of confidence that carried me through the next chapter of England, back again to Italy and finally home to Australia.

GRISELDA

When I returned to England, I stayed in Devon with a family my mother knew. Christina and Mark Reeve lived in a lovely old country house with three daughters and a son who was away painting. The Reeve rendezvous was like stepping out into another world – all my childhood fantasies life-size and ready to play. Every moment and experience fascinated me in a different way. Madam Reeve scared me a bit, but she gave me a good shove into their rich tapestry of life. Mark was quiet, but supportive when he could see me struggling to keep up, which was something I wanted so desperately! I loved the humour and poking fun, the fantastic stories – oh, gullible me. They fooled me so often. The three daughters were outdoor types and had me playing all sorts of new sports and games. There were night-time charades and introductions to their friends, ranging from witches to seven deaf men at one dinner party.

It was not until later in my stay I met James. He was at a nearby estate on commission to paint a portrait of Lady Farquar and he came back one night for dinner to meet me. I felt an immediate sense of compatibility with him. He had my kind of madness. James was responsible for bringing to life the 'Griselda' I had created years earlier in a real theatrical extravaganza. He decided to take me back with him as a very famous singer friend of his from some Baltic country to meet the Farquars and stay the weekend. James dressed me in a long ancient Chinese robe, with white ostrich feathers amid a number of hairpieces. He pinned passionflower to the low cut front of my robe, and gave me a black parasol and high heeled gold shoes. We arrived mid-morning to the gates of this huge Georgian mansion set in acres of land. Peacocks strutted around the garden as servants greeted us at the door. My heart was thumping, 'What was I doing here, and could I carry it off?'

James reassured me and then introduced me without looking my way in case he laughed. I draped myself against a couch and wall and spoke a little Greek and Ukrainian, learnt as a child. I was asked if I would like to change for dinner, and so I changed my hat for another one with a veil and two pheasant feathers sticking up two feet in the air. Bedtime came at last, and I was ushered into a huge room with a four-poster bed, but sleep would not come.

The whole weekend was a blur accentuated by a song I wrote for their Uncle Freddy, who must have been eighty. I sang it to him after dinner. Oddly, he disappeared and I never saw him again.

Uncle Freddy (Aged 75)

This song I composed
To entertain you,
You'll wonder at me
Before I am through,
You'll never enjoy life; as much as I do,
I will show you how.

I know all about you
But you don't know me,
Perhaps if you did

Banished I'd be,
But one thing is sure I can cook expertly,
I will show you how.

My beefsteaks and omelettes
Are loaded with spice,
And you haven't lived
Till you've tasted my rice,
But without my cooking
I'm still very nice,
I will show you how.

You wont regret it
And you won't resist,
Now I will show you
The things you have missed,
With a zip of your zipper, a flick of the wrist
I will show you how.

Age: nineteen

THE WAY TO A MAN'S HEART IS THROUGH HIS STOMACH

It was not long after my overseas trip that I met my future husband, Ian. I was still living on Robe Terrace, same old story, feeling very confident in my cooking, inspired to write songs and play guitar, but inadequate as a human being. An old friend from school days, who was now the most popular and attractive catch of the time, had lied to her boyfriend about being a magnificent cook. As she could not cook at all, in desperation she asked me if I would accompany her to a bachelor's pad, which her boyfriend shared with four other college students. She asked me to prepare a meal for all of them and pretend that it was her cooking.

I did all the preparation at home, and we both arrived late in the afternoon to their huge two-storey mansion. We were met by a very handsome bunch of men, my future husband being one of them. The inside of their pad proved to be pretty rough with not much furniture or cooking equipment. I managed to scrounge around and find an old beach towel to throw over a rickety old table. Of course I had candles, music and my food, which set the stage for a great night. No one knew our secret. I spent only a little time with any of the guests, though, as I had a job to do for my friend.

Six months later I met Ian at a party and we talked about his position as a ruckman for Port Adelaide, and his just-blossoming career as an architect. I pretended to love football, but was genuinely interested in architecture.

Visualise a large Roman banquet chamber, walls lined with rich purple hessian and draped with ivy, with gold plaster moulds of my mother's face gazing down onto a low, gold table piled with pomegranates and grapes. At the entrance there is an exotic wench in flowing white robes to wash one's feet with rose-scented water. She leads us to relax on the many couches that surround the table. A flute is playing and, through the doors, servants appear carrying huge trays laden with 'fruits from the sea', 'beasts from the plain' and wine from the vineyards high on the hills above Rome. Are we in Italy in the Roman era? No, we are in my parents' garage at Robe Terrace in the early 1960s. I am now twenty. My cooking skills had really developed and I had Ian as my catch.

My father paid for the event, my mother made it possible and my sister Jill was wench and coordinator. I was on menu and set-up. It was an engagement party to introduce my fiancé to Robe Terrace and the inner sanctuary of the Holden dynasty. I had painted flower vases gold for the wine and unfortunately each one held about half a bottle of wine. This meant everyone got drunk very quickly, as in the Roman times. Fortunately my parents never appeared at our parties, especially

Marriage, 1965

mine, and they did not approve of my engagement to a Port Adelaide footballer.

Before the night took a turn for the worse, the main meal was served – fresh oysters, fish wrapped in vine leaves, squid, octopus, chargrilled whole snapper, rosemary-encrusted lamb roast, suckling pig with sage butter and stuffed vegetables, and lastly syllabub for dessert. Much later when my mother came out to make sure everyone was leaving, she was dismayed to see her bed couches covered in red wine, and my fiancé was in disgrace for jumping on them and breaking one of the box bases. I was too sick to say goodnight to my guests. Worst of all, my very proper and quiet cousin from Melbourne was missing and later found in the wood shed with one of my friends.

Ian was a catch. He looked like Rock Hudson. He seemed a stable country boy, brought up in rural South Australia, but not from the stables of the 'upper crust'. This I loved. I wanted to escape from home to have babies and be hopelessly in love for the rest of my life. I had a totally unrealistic view of marriage, an obsessive love for Ian. He also brought a totally unrealistic approach to marriage. He started in private practice the day we got back from our honeymoon and immediately began working five days and five nights a week.

Lucky I had my time taken up with restoring an old cottage. Lucky I had all of Ian's business friends to entertain. Lucky I got a job as wholesale and retail manager for a clothing outlet, Norma Tullo's, despite having no knowledge of the industry or of how to balance the books. I learned very quickly and had to run the place on my own. There were many nights I had to stay back to work it all out. What does this say about my lack of school education? It showed me very clearly that I could do anything if I set my heart to it. During these first few years of marriage, before my children were born, I had many creative opportunities and diversions to keep me busy.

UNDER-THE-TABLE AND OVER-THE-TOP PARTIES

Although I was busy with my full-time job in the fashion industry, it did not stop me from creating feasts, even for the two of us. Before Nicholas was born we used to have bed parties, and I continued having them for the rest of my life. In our old house in the smart suburb of Gilberton, the only place it was warm was in bed. There were really funny times like when béarnaise sauce was splashed all over our new curtains or the time we hid a roast dinner under the sheets when someone came to call unexpectedly. On pre-dinner party nights I had Ian in bed with our TV dinner, peeling and pipping grapes for grape brulee. I would bring our evening meals from downstairs on trays until we could afford to renovate, and then did I go to town.

The main areas of focus were the kitchen and dining room, both riddled with salt damp. The dining room was my masterpiece. Black beams panelled the walls to cover salt repair and on the ceilings I painted huge nudes, Michelangelo style, floating in a blue sky, and a cornucopia loaded with fruit. Ian loved my cooking. When his architectural practice took off after he had finished with football, he had to focus ninety per cent on his new business. I spent my time entertaining at home for his business friends where I was able to be more extravagant than usual. I loved planning the menu and the effort of getting it all together and cooking it.

I was often worn out from all the preparation, frequently had too many drinks, and grew sick of the chitchat, at which point I just wanted to find a quiet place. Under my mother's old oak dining table was the spot. I had spent some time under it even when it was still at Robe Terrace. It had four large pillars and room to relax and it was nice and dark. I used to do this in other people's houses as well when I got sick of the show. Occasionally someone else would follow suit. I recall a chap I knew pretty well but had never taken to who came down under the table one time and took his penis out. At that moment there just happened to be the silver cap of a champagne bottle on the floor beside me, which I firmly stuck on the end of his penis, squeezing in the wire so he couldn't get it off. I bet he never tried that again!

There were other under-the-table parties that were subversive and sneaky. I did not sit at the table long enough to experience them myself, but they were to do with hands and feet and far more serious in their intent – hanky-panky. Then there were the over-the-top parties – when someone actually lay on the table when it was loaded with glasses and crockery, or danced on the table, sometimes with very few clothes on. I have absolute innocence in this area of party antics, and I have no need to reveal those who played the over-the-top games.

However, there is one person who needs to be revealed because she has played such an important role throughout my life: Judy Hardy. She was an artist and a professional party and food planner and, at that stage, the wife of a mad Irish psychiatrist. Many times, Judy and I were hostesses of grand affairs. We met during the 1970s due to the very

over the top and under the table partys

difficult births of our children, and subsequent tragedies ensured our relationship flourished. Judy was also director of mental health and directed mine. I joined Judy in Morocco for her sixtieth birthday, where she just happened to be buying and selling houses. What a show! The celebration was a movie of colour and creativity lasting three weeks. Survival, changing pace and reinvention with a creative overview have kept Judy and I connected right up to now.

THE TROUBLE WITH MARRIAGE

Ian just could not cope with the pressure of work, and the pressure of marriage and me. One had to suffer and, although the futility of it all did not really set in until years later, the pattern was established in the first month. Deep down I felt Ian did not take me seriously and I had to hide my feelings. I started up my old antics again – running through the streets with no clothes on, or throwing dice and giving myself outlandish and challenging options based on the result. This approach to life I took on after enjoying Luke Rhinehart's *The Dice Man*, which is well worth a read.

In the middle of the night I climbed in through my friends' second-storey window, wet and cold, after having jumped in their pool. I crept very carefully into bed with them while they slept, without waking them. They were certainly surprised to see me in the morning. There were many other similar experiences that have faded from memory, best forgotten. What seems incredible to me now is that despite my provocative and blatant manner, never once did I take a step further than exhibitionism. Opportunities to explore my fading sexual responses were never tested.

During this time I did an interior design course, and got involved with Ian working on some of his projects. I often said, 'If you can't beat them, join them.' I learnt transcendental meditation with Ian, worked like a man in the house and garden and then became perfect hostess for his business clients.

Sadly, though, it seemed there was to be an ominous repetition of the past. Ian triggered memories of my father in many ways. Both never expressed their love, which made me resort to outlandish behaviour. I kept myself busy doing things, waiting for the time when Ian would say, 'I don't care what you do, I still love you.'

Ian really did appreciate my doing. In fact he encouraged it. But my desire to be appreciated as a woman in the physical, sensual and emotional area failed dismally. I encountered excuses and denials from him, and my plaintive pleas at the beginning became a monotonous whine with flare-ups of anger and then silent withdrawal. It was then I decided to get pregnant. A baby would be the answer to everything. I was sick through the whole nine months but, after an extremely difficult two-day birth, Nicholas arrived.

I was delighted with Nicholas, such a small living creature and so beautiful. I couldn't believe he was all mine. Days and months flashed by. I was fully occupied with the job of motherhood when I had a second awful pregnancy – 'definitely the last' – and Eliza was born. I had the perfect pair. Just as our new house was near completion, Ian decided we should try out high-rise living in some apartments he had designed at the beach. They were selling far too slowly, and the penthouse at the top was vacant. Ian convinced me that being next to the beach would mean the whole seashore would become the children's garden. But what he didn't consider was the impact of a ten-story apartment and a feeling of isolation that would impact on a new mother with two very young children. I was hoping the move would improve the struggling marriage. The novelty lasted six months.

HELL ON EARTH

Ian had long trips away to Kangaroo Island, and big work projects on. Nicholas got very bad impetigo and poor medical advice left him with his whole body covered with eczema. Eliza developed an abscess in her ear and one lunchtime I found her slumped over in her highchair unconscious. I panicked. I did not know what to do. There was no one around to help. She looked blue. I didn't even know how to give her mouth-to-mouth resuscitation. Fortunately she came around in a couple of minutes. I called the doctor and she was taken to hospital with suspected meningitis. What a relief when the tests were clear and she was sent home. But still something was not right. She exhibited peculiar behaviour and would throw her head back. More consultation with the doctor reassured me there was nothing wrong. I went to a second doctor who said she had acute bronchitis and gave her a shot of penicillin. One hour after this she was dead.

Sick children had been a perpetual fear for me, but to have a child die, our child, did not seem possible. I went into shock. I was in isolation. No one was around. My parents and Ian were over on Kangaroo Island. My sisters and friends were on the other side of town. Here I was with the caretaker, collapsed on his bed that smelt of urine. Eventually Ian and my parents arrived. The steps taken after that are just a blur, but one thing is clear now: I did not care that my sisters were not there. They hardly knew Eliza anyway. I cursed the move to Glenelg and Ian's frequent trips away. Also I blamed myself, even though I took Eliza to two different doctors on the three days before her death.

Eliza's funeral said it all. For some reason it took place in the largest chapel at Centennial Park, which seated hundreds. There were just six of us: me, Ian, my parents, Helen and Andy Brown, who had been the only support I had in Eliza's health issues the weeks before she died. An unknown entity gave the eulogy. A waste of empty words. Watching the little white coffin disappear slowly into the ground was the last straw. Even now I cannot explain why this tragedy was dealt with in such an impersonal way. It was no one's fault. It was just how it was. I locked my grief away inside of me for years, talked to no one, and no one suggested any professional help.

After all that, it got worse. We ended up in Sydney at an architectural convention and subsequently had a car accident in the CBD – but there was one miracle. I got pregnant with Rachel in that same week as Eliza's funeral. Though it was a miracle, it was also too soon after Eliza's death. I could not accept a new life while I was still in shock. My system was a mess, and the next eight months were hell. Rachel was born after a near caesarean.

Three months later I was rushed to hospital with thyrotoxicosis and a horribly high pulse rate. I was sedated for two weeks and then sent home to stay in bed for four months before they could operate. I couldn't properly look after Rachel and had to have live-in help. The live-in help happened to be a screwed-up woman who caused more trouble than she was worth. No sooner was this all over than Rachel developed throat infections that caused her to convulse. We had just moved house again, and she was in and out of hospital. Fear of what had happened to Eliza made my ability to cope far worse. In fact, if it had not been for Ian, I would not have coped at all. He was wonderful. Night after night we had to sponge Rachel down and nothing was too much trouble for him. He was an excellent nurse to us all. During those awful years there was so much sickness and no end to fear and worry.

The end did come when I was sent to a specialist after continual bouts of throat infections. He talked to me at length about my life and to my surprise put me on a course of antidepressants. I was fascinated, as two months later all symptoms had gone. I felt terrific. The specialist sent me to a therapist to find a cause, but it was obvious. I wanted attention and I got it from Ian when I was ill. We had sessions for both of us to try and find a solution. It seemed we both wanted a continuation of the marriage, but unless Ian could find a way to balance his work with family commitments there was not much hope.

BACK TO KANGAROO ISLAND

Rachel, the second daughter I had prayed for, started her life as a sickly baby freaking us all out with high temperatures and convulsions. Fortunately she turned into a robust and healthy child once we returned to Kangaroo Island to live. It was Ian's idea to move to the island. He believed that if he could work in town three days with no distractions, he could spend the rest of the week with us. It would separate his work from his personal life. We agreed. It seemed the perfect solution.

At first it was healing for us all. I loved those early years. I loved the discovery and nature of my children. With them I could be a child again and have experiences I never had at Robe Terrace. The beach was our playground, our vegetable garden and kitchen; the source of hours of playing with food, and the setting for bonfire feasts at night.

I also became coordinator of a community program I created with some teachers from the school. Playgroups commenced and we all got involved. Nicholas took an hour bus ride to the local school, while Rachel stayed home and spent long hours on the beach with me. Life seemed pretty wonderful on all levels. The therapist gave us hope that the move would heal our marriage. It didn't. It separated us even more.

Ian helped and worked with me for the first six months but the temptation of a new job made his trips to Adelaide more frequent. One day, he arrived home to inform me he was going overseas for seven weeks. It was the last straw. I was furious and upset – nothing seemed to have changed. Ian's basic impulses were still self-motivated. I did not want to sign the papers that would allow him to go. But of course I did. He left me in a state of self-pity and despair.

To top it off, at the same time there was a mouse plague on the island that was so bad mice were running around my bed and nibbling at my fingers. One even crawled up my leg waking me from sleep. The children thought it was terrific. They made all sorts of devices for catching them. The mice walked a plank to get some cheese until they slipped into buckets of water the children had set up. The mice swam around squealing till they drowned.

I felt trapped. There was no relief from mothering, house maintenance, failing pressure pumps, water restrictions, electricity blackouts and living in a community that was very hard to break into.

I developed a back problem and convinced myself I was about to be put in a wheelchair. I rushed to town to see my therapist, shedding hysterical tears and expressing my feelings of failure regarding our move from town. I could not accept Ian's major goal in life of professional excellence. If the therapist had got his head out of his arse he would have said it was time for me to get out then. I knew he could see little hope in the marriage's continuation. Instead he was waiting for me to say it myself, but I was so frightened and confused it did not enter my head that I had a choice. The only things I remember clearly from that awful day were the words he said as he led me to the door: 'Have you ever thought of having an affair?'

LEAD PIPE LOUIE

Lead Pipe Louie acquired her name after an SP bookie didn't want to pay her winning bet. She left angrily, saying, 'I'll be back!' She returned with a huge chunk of plumber's lead pipe hidden in her silver Oroton bag. 'If you don't pay me,' she said, 'I'll hit you.' Which she did, breaking all his teeth!

That was long before I met her. At that time, she was married into a traditional southern Italian family and business. I think in those early days, protection was a matter of course. I liked the name as it suited her forthright approach to life. Louie did not mince words and could pull a mean punch if need be. But in all the years I have known her one thing stands out, and that's her implicit fairness in the way she treats people and life.

I had heard of her psychic abilities through word-of-mouth and I had been fascinated with metaphysics since childhood. Louie was short and round with bright pink cheeks, corn-coloured hair and bright blue eyes with painted-on dark eyebrows, always a different shape and colour. Her only gypsy element was her flamboyant clothes and jewellery.

She grew up in the north of South Australia in a house made of wheat bags and lime. She had a simple uncomplicated life, which I loved

Louie

hearing about. It was so unlike mine, which seemed to have far too many issues I couldn't deal with, and a family I didn't feel comfortable with.

I went to see her nearing the end of our marriage for some advice. Louie had an ongoing effect on my personal, creative, and professional life over the next thirty years – I would be dead or in a mental institution if not for Louie leading me out of each disaster before I led myself into the next. She gave me insight, guidance and unconditional love, something I had never experienced before. She put out options, and words of wisdom in my business decisions, certainly with the use of her well-worn cards. But more important was her personal insight. She became my best friend, my teacher, sometimes my mother and father. And all the time I could use her to tap into my fascination with metaphysics. She didn't read; she was not the least bit materialistic; she didn't intellectualise; she just knew. She became part of my children's lives and mine. Our friendship sometimes is almost impossible to explain. The process of getting to know Louie gave me an understanding of the importance of balance in my life. Louie is still here, still relevant, and still big. We are friends with a mutual and respectful understanding.

CHAPTER 3

Mains

Gnocchi à la romana

SERVES 6

INGREDIENTS

1 litre milk*
½ teaspoon grated nutmeg
1–1¼ cups semolina
2 egg yolks
100 g grated parmesan
60 g melted butter
Salt and pepper

METHOD

In a non-stick saucepan, heat up the milk and nutmeg until about to boil.

Slowly add semolina, whisking as you go. The mixture will thicken. On a low heat, slowly stir for 5 minutes.

Take off the heat, then add the egg yolks, the parmesan and the butter and mix until smooth.

Turn mixture out onto a piece of baking paper. Make a sphere about 20 cm high.

Let mixture cool.

With a medium size cookie cutter, cut out rounds using up the leftovers by forming extra rounds.

Place rounds into a baking dish lined with baking paper and sprinkle with parmesan, a little knob of butter and cook in a heated 180°C oven for 20 minutes.

* I often add flavours such as sage, rosemary or thyme into the milk when I am heating it. If you do this, the herbs need to be strained off before you reheat the milk just before boiling point.

Nick's handmade potato gnocchi with rosa sauce

SERVES 4 TO 6

INGREDIENTS

GNOCCHI

1 kg large potatoes, peeled, quartered and steamed till very soft
2 egg yolks
Salt and pepper
150 g (approx.) strong 00 plain flour

ROSA SAUCE

4 large cloves garlic, finely chopped
3 tablespoons olive oil
6–8 large, very ripe tomatoes, roughly chopped into 2 cm pieces
Salt and pepper
1 bunch basil, chopped (keep a third aside to garnish)
1 good teaspoon sugar, if needed
Good splash cream (or 2 dollops)
Fresh parmesan or pecorino cheese, grated

METHOD

To make the gnocchi, let potatoes cool and mash well in bowl till creamy. Add the yolks, salt and pepper and mix well.

Slowly add flour, mixing until the mixture starts to form a very soft, wet dough. Tip dough out onto floured table and continue mixing in remaining flour, bit by bit, until just workable* so that you can section it off and roll it into finger-thickness snakes.

Using a knife, cut the 'snakes' into 1.5–2 cm pieces at an angle to form the gnocchi. Using the back of the knife, pick up the gnocchi and place side-by-side on a floured tray. Do not pile on top of each other. Continue until all the dough is used.

To make the sauce, in a medium-sized deep frypan, lightly cook garlic in oil for 3 minutes. Do not brown.

Add tomatoes, salt, pepper and two thirds of the basil.

Simmer on low for 10 to 15 minutes and taste for sweetness** and then simmer for another 10 to 15 minutes until sauce thickens.

Before serving, add the cream and bring up temperature without boiling.

To serve, fill a very large pot*** with water, a splash of olive oil and a pinch of salt. Bring to a boil.

Add gnocchi to boiling water and when all of them start to float, wait 30 seconds before draining and tossing gnocchi with the rosa sauce.

Garnish with fresh basil and grated parmesan.

* Dough should feel soft to touch when rolling, but not tacky. This will make light and fluffy gnocchi. If you add more flour, it will feel firmer like bread dough, and will make a firmer gnocchi.

** If your tomatoes are not sweet, you may need to add a little sugar to balance out the acidity.

*** If you don't have a big pot, cook the gnocchi in two batches as they only take a few minutes to cook.

LUCIA'S READY-MADE FRESH GNOCCHI

When you cannot be bothered cooking, go to Lucia's at the Central Market, purchase fresh, ready-made gnocchi and add your own choice of sauce.

Fish bake

SERVES 4

INGREDIENTS

1 large potato
2 tablespoons butter
1 onion
½ bulb fennel
2 sticks celery
4 x 400 g tins whole peeled tomatoes
2 tail ends of salmon (it's thinner)
1 lemon, sliced thinly

METHOD

Boil potato until soft.

Heat butter in a frypan and sauté the chopped onion, fennel and celery.

Lay out sliced boiled potato in ovenproof dish, and spread over onion mix.

Slice tomatoes and lay on top.

Bake vegetables, covered, in hot oven (180°C) until heated through.

Place fish on top of vegetables and add lemon slices to top of fish

Re-cover and bake in oven for approx. 20 mins.

Ceviche tostadita

SERVES 4

INGREDIENTS

100 g of fresh King George whiting or other fresh white skinless fish
3 limes
1/10 white onion
1 tablespoon soft brown sugar
2 teaspoons Maldon sea salt
1 red chilli (optional)
¼ ruby grapefruit
1 cm fresh jalapeño
5 sprigs coriander
¼ Spanish onion, finely diced (cut as small as possible)
1 reed avocado
Bite-size white round corn tortillas*
1 fresh fennel bulb, shaved
Pinch toasted cumin seeds

METHOD

Remove any bones or skin from fish. Dice fish finely with a sharp knife and set aside in fridge until all other elements of dish is ready.

Make the lime dressing that will eventually cook the fish. Zest half 1 lime into a small bowl. Add juice of 2 limes. Add white onion, soft brown sugar and salt. Add a pinch of chopped red chilli if you like things spicy.

Cut rind and skin from grapefruit and segment so that there is no pith on wedges. Cut each segment into 4 or 5 fine strips. Note you will only need about 2 segments of fruit so keep the rest for something else.

Make guacamole by blending fresh jalapeño, coriander and Spanish onion. Add paste to avocado and mash with a fork, juice of remaining lime and salt to taste. Set aside.

Fry tortillas in hot oil until golden. Drain well.

Remove fish from fridge and add enough of lime dressing to cover all of the fish. Gently move fish through marinade with your fingers.

With a teaspoon, add a layering of guacamole to fried tortillas.

Remove fish from dressing and sprinkle on top of guacamole

Add tiny drop of olive oil to shaved fennel with a few toasted cumin seeds crushed between your fingers and pinch of salt. Put a few strands on top of fish and top with a few tiny pieces of grapefruit

Serve straight away.

* You can buy these from specialty shops – Chile Mojo in Adelaide sells them. Use thin bruschetta toasts if tortillas are unavailable.

MOUNTAIN MAN

He came down from the hill with a goat he had just killed. It was another one of those weeks on Kangaroo Island when I was alone. Ian was overseas, my children were at school, my house on the cliff was the eyeglass through which I could watch the sea and sky – but I did not see them. The grey colour of my thoughts and gradually fading dreams clouded my vision. The hopelessness of my marriage was something I found difficult to accept.

As he expertly sectioned up the craggy beast that had trodden the cliffs above the sea, I just sat and watched. He was a slim dark young man with a beard and I thought, 'I don't really want a goat, and I don't really want to talk, but I can't be rude.' So as usual lots of, 'Oh, how lovely, thank you. I just love goat. Coffee?' I had met Mountain Man (MM) once before with his wife. They had moved to the island from America to settle – he to continue his nature photography books and his wife to help run his small retail outlet in Kingscote. He talked for a short while then left.

The next week, MM came over again with more bounty from the land and after the usual polite words, I offered him a coffee and he sat down on the floor with me and talked about his life and travels around the world. His father was a taxidermist and an animal trainer for motion pictures or, as MM put it, 'one son of a bitch'. His father had taken him on many expeditions. MM later went on his own expeditions and spent many months living on Native American reservations and wandering the world as a nomad.

My dull brain slightly stirred to hear of his adventures but my overwhelming feeling was still resentment of his intrusion into my loneliness and my personal space. I couldn't hide or easily disappear from his unpredictable visits, which soon became weekly. I continued to listen, and gradually I began to warm to his sensitive consideration and some sort of understanding I felt he had for me. Nothing was personal. Nothing was suggestive; no smart word of flattery, only experiences of life, nature and animals.

The view from the house as seen through his eyes changed my perception dramatically. For the first time I could feel life all around me – the wind's moods, the sky and changing patterns of the sea. Our observations took us further away from the hilltop house, along the cliffs, into the scrub and along the coastline. Indifference in him turned to curiosity. I developed a fascination in what he knew and what he could teach me. One afternoon we squatted on the ground and watched an echidna on its back. We watched for the half an hour it took the creature to turn over. Everything was so easy in the bush with MM. He found food, found his way, while watching what went on around us – it may have been an eagle soaring in the sky, rock lichens, species of animals and birds.

MM never talked about his wife and I never talked about Ian, yet when Ian came down for weekends the four of us would get together and have a great time. I didn't know if MM had told his wife of his visits and I didn't ask. I didn't bother to tell Ian because I didn't think he would be very interested.

It was six months after our first meeting and the four of us were sitting by the fire after dinner that our feet touched. It was like an electric shock, and although the encounter of two toes seemed a pathetic attempt at contact, the implications were very real. I looked straight into his dark eyes and felt the vibrancy, and then the moment passed. One evening a couple of days later he came and as soon as I saw him I knew what was ahead. Terror overwhelmed me. I could not cope with the unveiling of my body, my inhibitions, and my miserable self-esteem. I wanted to escape before it was too late. Still, six months of gentle encouragement from MM had made me realise that going back to emptiness would be worse than the difficult step ahead. Only his consideration, his tenderness and gentle coaxing made our first sexual encounter a small spark of pleasure, instead of a nightmare.

That man gently lifted me out of the gloom of my negative sexual disposition and made me feel I was not such an awful failure. His patience was endless, his insight and my reticence deep and profound. I didn't have to explain – he knew.

A year of discovery followed, but surprisingly no one discovered us. MM left before the sun came up. His wife thought he was out bush, and the last thing Ian would presume was that I was having an affair. The weeks took on a new meaning. I would see MM almost every day and sometimes two nights in a row, and if I went to town he would go too. We would meet at the market and buy our supplies and head for the hills or beach. Nights were spent in old pubs on country roads, a world apart from everyone. We were two thirsty animals who had found an oasis in each other. He unleashed creative energy in me I have never experienced since. Wonderful things happened – poetry and music poured out of nowhere and even captured the imagination of an American promoter who in the space of a week set up recording studios and musicians to make a master tape to send to Los Angeles.

From complete indifference at the beginning, now I had an obsession to grab every moment that I could. He wanted to expose our relationship but, even though we talked at great length of one day living together, it was just a dream to me. The reality of what the truth would do did not occur to me until the night that everything was exposed. The four of us were having dinner together and in a moment of silence I heard MM's words telling it all. I could not believe it was happening. Ian was amazed and horrified; MM wife's mood was silent acceptance, and the look on MM's face one of satisfaction and relief. Suddenly I had to face the pain, the deception and the truth. The months ahead were hell.

So many words tumbled from Ian's lips: communications I'd wanted to hear for so long. He wrote me letters I could not understand, or did not believe or accept. It was too late. In every way, Ian and my extended family tried to reason with me. Nothing would change my mind. Maybe if I had seen the effect it had on my family, I would have reconsidered. My father and mother would not speak to me; family conferences took place while I sat alone in the Cliff House deciding the fate of my children if I ran away with MM. I had never considered that my children would not always be with me! But the picture just got worse. I could not run from anyone. I was not allowed to stay on Kangaroo Island. It was decided that Ian would take over our place on the island on the condition he helped find a place in Adelaide for the children and me. He did.

Palmer Place was a condemned cottage that hadn't been lived in for seven years and it suited me, as I was a condemned woman. MM came often to visit, waiting for the moment when I would be free to be with him. I found that the strain of children at a new school and the awful guilt and loss of Kangaroo Island were all too much. I could feel myself slipping away from MM and the island memories.

The break-up of my marriage had exposed the raw reality of my true character. Once I took away all the trappings of secret love and childish games, I had to face who I really was.

Rainbows and Dewdrops (for MM)

Rainbows and dewdrops, sunlight through rain,
Night sky and moon glow, never the same,
Silence that comforts, awareness that grew,
These are the thoughts that remind me of you.

Storm clouds and sunsets, wind in the night,
Mist on the hills in the first morning light,
Looks that mean so much are just but a few,
Of some of the things that remind me of you.

Wetness on smooth rocks, patterns of sun,
Shadows of darkness, when night has begun,
Soft lips that touch me, and warm me right through,
These are the things that remind me of you.

Firelight and candles, sleep is not far,
My spirit will find you, wherever you are,
In your other world, there is one thing still free,
And these are the thoughts that remind you of me.

Age: thirty-two

THE FUNERAL PARLOUR

It seems I had a lot to say about my father in the years leading up to my marriage to Ian, but not so much to say after that time. I had escaped from him. I was no longer under his control and I had trained Ian to be the son he expected. He had nothing to criticise. Ian had become a respected architect and was no longer a Port Adelaide footballer. He had of course a connection with my children too, but I could sense the same pattern of control he wanted with them, so I kept visitation to a minimum. But after many stints of pneumonia, my father ended up with bone cancer. My mother was a dedicated carer right to the end, and the end came in a palliative care hospice, where he was permitted to have a dose of brandy every four hours and wear his sarong.

I never had any kind or loving words from him except for the last time I went to visit him. As I left his room, the last words I ever heard from him were, 'You look very pretty and no buts!'.

The next time I saw him, he was in a coffin in the mortuary. I had never wanted to see a dead body but the children for some strange reason asked if they could see 'Boppa' one more time and my mother agreed. So the three of us went together. We walked in to find the coffin on the ground and open. Nick sauntered over while Rachel skipped around his body. He looked tiny. He was not the massive frame and bellowing voice usually towering above us. Nick peered in, and then bent over and very firmly pressed down on his nose and then walked away. I was in shock. The symbolic message did not come to me until quite a while later. It was, 'You are down there, and we are up here.'

The physicality and dominance was over. The piercing blue eyes were shut. But as I was to find out, the emotional residue remained for years, until I sought therapy and found an element of forgiveness. But I never really forgot.

Many years after my father's death I found out things about his character that I wished I had learned earlier. He was wild and reckless as a boy and teenager; a practical joker, an accident-prone adventurer. He sounded like me. I wish I had seen that fun side of him. He used to ride his motorbike around the dining room and stand on top of the door. He tormented his sister Nell by putting electric currents under the chairs of her boyfriends. Nell never got married.

BELINDA'S RESTAURANT

I ran away from marriage,
I ran away from home,
I had to start my life afresh,
With children on my own,
I had to look for answers,
I had to find a way,
I had no education,
And had far too much to say.
But I had an inclination,
Followed by intent,.
Fostered by a friend of mine,
A miracle he sent,
He had one thing to say to me,
One thing that I could do,
Something that could save my life,
And carry me right through.
'YOU CAN COOK!'

Age: thirty-four

My life on Kangaroo Island and my marriage were over. I was sitting at the Old Lion Hotel in North Adelaide with an old 'foodie' friend of mine called Ron Tremaine, who had just taken over the hotel. It was the late 1970s. I had no income and felt desperate, guilty and friendless since leaving Ian. Friends had taken sides; mostly Ian's side. I felt I was sinking in quicksand. There was no one to hold my hand and pull me out until Ron Tremaine appeared. I still can't believe Ron would become such a mentor and friend to me with no strings attached. He literally held my hand as he presented me with an idea and helped me execute it. I could never have invented or executed it on my own.

Meanwhile, my two children were dragged away from Kangaroo Island to a new school and a derelict house, and were not fully informed or aware that Ian and I had separated, as past history had taught them that it was not unusual for their dad to be somewhere else. Nothing was different. Now he was working on Kangaroo Island and I was in Adelaide.

My mother outside Palmer Place, location of Belinda's Restaurant

Palmer Place was a complete wreck, but had a special vibe and great potential and was in a fantastic position. It had parkland frontage and was a ten-minute walk to the CBD. It was tiny, about ten metres wide. There were two bedrooms upstairs, a small narrow staircase, a tiny bathroom on a little landing with no separate toilet, and stairs down to another two rooms underneath. There was no kitchen, and a narrow north-facing garden running down one side of the house, full of weeds. The block continued down to a car access at the end of a lane, so there was room to build on a kitchen and a large sunny living area facing north.

Before the renovation, however, it was impossible to imagine the culinary possibilities of my life, when all we had was a bar fridge and a muffin toaster. Nick and Rachel had already been inventive using this tiny little cooker in all sorts of creative ways, but we were months away from a proper kitchen. In the end, old friends Judy and Peter McGill offered us the use of a little flat at the back of their house just around the corner from the children's new school. It was a miracle Judy and Peter returned to my life and I will be indebted to them forever. I had a chance to get the renovation underway, and we were able to get a dog, Chloe, for the children. Chloe was a pivotal part of our lives in and around Palmer Place. At last renovations were done, and we had a garden recreated by a young landscape gardener who put magic into this tiny suburban backyard.

With Ron's support, Belinda's Restaurant was born. It was a private eating house that could seat twelve people around the beautiful oak table and chairs I had inherited from my mother. But how could this work? There was no urinal, no council approval as such, but permission gained by means of permits given by the licensing court to serve liquor on specific nights for up to twelve people. It was BYO and a set menu designed by the host and me. It seemed like a bizarre idea, but Ron was an entrepreneur, and a mover and shaker, so I listened carefully to what he had to say. Ron planned everything and invited the first VIP guests for a demo run. I was in charge of menu design, cooking and service.

These were the years of silver service, five courses, and extravaganza. This was the time to put all my past dinner experiences and dinner party knowledge to the test. But this time guests would be paying for the experience and it was all taking place in a four-roomed cottage with one bathroom, no separate lavatory and a four-by-three kitchen. The renovation did mean that this little space could spill out into the family room that now had windows looking out onto an instant silver birch forest, pond and fountain. This design meant that my children had somewhere else to live other than their bedrooms, and on the nights of my dinners, the guests could have a drink in this lovely space before sitting down at the table. My children and dog Chloe had to be out of the way upstairs, where they played boxing with their socks on their hands, and other fairly quiet activities.

Ron picked the first group of guests, who were all people in food and hospitality. I selected the menu. Hors d'oeuvres first, and a selection of cold antipasto ideas, things that seem old hat now. After the hors d'oeuvres, I served a hot or cold soup, an entrée, sorbet, main course and sweets. My mother, who had got over the shock of my separation, was the waitress. She had moved back to Adelaide from Kangaroo Island after my father died and was looking for something to do.

The demo was a huge success. Everyone there booked a party of his or her own. I was completely overwhelmed. So started the life of Belinda's Restaurant. Open for three nights a week, it was very much repeat clientele, so I had to become innovative with the menu. Sprinkled through these bookings was a selection of the rich, famous and artistic – premier of the day Don Dunstan; Len Evans, wine magnate; the infamous Alan Bond, who gave me a $200 tip; and entertainers, like the cast of *Hair*.

PUPPY POO, WHAT TO DO?

It was the very first dinner after the demo run, and the guests were a group from the country. We had just got our new puppy Chloe. Of course Chloe was put outside once the guests arrived. The guests insisted the puppy be let in. I was not aware that she had gone for a look in the dining room and unbeknown to us all, did a circle of sloppy poo under the table. The guests sat down only to discover two minutes later, all of their shoes were covered in puppy poo. There we all were out in the garden with the garden hose and a brush, cleaning it off. Luckily they thought it was a great joke, maybe helped along by the pre-dinner drinks already consumed in the kitchen.

As time went by and I got to know groups very well, the occasions turned into 'events', which was an experience as well as a meal. I became the creator of fantasies in food and theming, starting with a dinner for Judy Barnes, whose son David was murdered in Adelaide in the 1970s. She joined with other victims of crime to meet at my place for their special dinners. As they came so often, I had to invent new ways to entertain them, so I developed cultural-themed dinners. I cannot recall the menus, but I certainly remember the process. My Japanese first course was set up in the children's playroom – cushions on the floor, all black and red with traditional Japanese fare and me in a kimono. Second course was French with Parisian scenes on the walls of the dining room, me in a little French maid outfit and frilly apron. There was I in the kitchen cooking, serving, then upstairs for a change of costume for the next course. The funniest was the next course. Nick and Rachel were dressed in loincloths carrying drums and covered with luminous paint. They asked the guests to follow them to the beat of their drums – out of the dining room and out the front door down the road to the laneway and in the back gate. Imagine twelve grownups marching up the street behind two painted half-naked children. In the back garden the children performed a little ceremony while I put on the next costume and prepared the Moroccan course and served it in the now Moroccan-decorated dining room. Last was the 'Aussie' dessert in the garden grotto – orange toffee, macadamia nuts and preserved ginger, with me in a costume of jeans, a Holden T-shirt, pigtails and an Akubra hat.

I did this all with no help. The guests had simply requested they look after their own wine, if I could manage the rest by myself. Never again! It took a week to recover.

KUNG FU CHICKEN BREASTS

Visualise a grand silver service luncheon, with twelve Adelaide aristocrats. We served a feast of sumptuous hors d'oeuvres, my special smoked salmon roulade, gin and watermelon sorbet, and, for main, stuffed chicken breast with a lemon, mustard and cheese sauce. My mother was ahead of me in the slow track around the table with the chicken. I followed not far behind with the vegetables. No one other than my mother really knew how to handle the spoons and the reaching around aspect of silver service. It usually takes a long time to learn this skill. However, on this occasion I needed all the time there was, as Mum suddenly discovered we were one breast short.

I went straight into rescue mode. First, I whispered to Mum to go even slower around the table with the vegetables while I went back to the kitchen. The rest of the chicken breasts were frozen. I went into Kung Fu mode and with brute strength that came from nowhere, I tore a frozen breast off the rest, ran it under hot water, bashed the shit out of it, patted it dry, then into the pan, sauced and piping hot, in perfect time for my mother who was coming to get me and what she hoped was the last breast to go on the plate. Patting my brow, I slid back into the dining room as if nothing unexpected had happened.

My very naughty regulars demanded an evening of 'rude' food, which definitely gave expression to my over-the-top tendancies, about which people, especially family, had often said, 'Belinda, now you have gone too far!'

Rude Food Menu

FIRST COURSE
Spunk soup – potato and leek soup

ENTRÉE
Arsehole, vagina and clitoris stew – snails, baby squid and baby rice noodle stew

MAINS
Genitalia – prawns, new potatoes cooked in red food colouring to look like wrinkled balls with penis carrots

DESSERT
Huge cream caramel breasts with red jelly nipples and a fence of cocks and balls made with choux pastry filled with cream and grated chocolate

Of course the guest of honour bit the red nipples off at first glance.

By now I had to get some extra help. My mother had decided that the long nights were not for her. I found the most perfect person for the job by word-of-mouth. Barb was colourful, hardworking and a real character. Everyone loved her. She came at seven and left at ten-thirty, and then I had to carry on with coffee, until I scooped everyone out the door far later than I would have wished.

One night, I was suddenly out of business. The Adelaide City Council (ACC) rang all my guests (who had booked and paid licence court fees) and told them that their permits were not valid. Ron and I were led to believe that as long as we had the permits, all was okay, but on the contrary, we should have consulted the ACC first.

My hands were tied. All I could do was close and seek legal advice, and I also had to seek other employment. I became a gardener then a picture framer until the planning appeals tribunal was over. After one year, I was granted the right to resume my business in my home.

Belinda's Restaurant was famous now, so to speak, which put pressure on a business that combined commerce, pleasure and family life in a four-roomed cottage. There were no weekends, it was difficult for me to have any personal life, and it was restrictive for the children. They certainly ate well, but I felt their education suffered from my lack of involvement. They did not embrace the academic world, and I did not push them. As I felt guilty for leaving my marriage, I wanted to be their best friend as well as their mother, which turned out to be a bit of a mistake. Anyway, Belinda's Restaurant came to an end when I met and fell in love with a new man.

In the early years at Palmer Place it was tough for the children. Nothing was properly explained to them about Ian and me separating, they disliked their new school, and I was busy renovating and looking for a job. Thank goodness for Rachel's drum kit, Chloe the dog, and Bimbo, the horse tethered in the parklands. Their transition to secondary school was also a failure. I didn't want a repeat of my Wilderness school experiences and bad memories, so I settled on Pembroke, which I had heard catered for students interested in the arts . . . wrong! The headmistress suggested that it might be better if Nick left at sixteen, though Rachel struggled on.

Our divorce proceedings were very civilised. Ian and I had a joint female lawyer, and it all seemed very easygoing as I left the family courts saying to Ian, 'Thank you for having me.' We had decided to leave the Cliff House in our joint names, thinking we could very happily share. At the time, Ian had settled himself into Kangaroo Island to live and work there, and I had settled into Palmer Place with the children.

There were some good times at Palmer Place, playing harmless silly games like going to the shop in our pyjamas before getting all tucked up in my bed ready to watch the next episode of *Roots*. We would purchase Snickers and have competitions of whose lasted the longest. We would go sliding on ice blocks down Montefiore Hill – off to the ice works, wheel the big blocks to the hill, with towels to sit on, and race each other to the bottom. We made home videos of mystery murders in the little garden with their friends. Usually in the story one of them would end up drowning in the pond.

Later, when they were in their teens, I gave up my house to the children. I built a hexagonal mud house, eight metres square, at the bottom of the garden and lived there whenever I came back to Adelaide from Kangaroo Island. My children had to look after themselves, and they had to deal with me. I really did think I was doing an excellent job as their mother, friend and playmate. This was a big mistake. I only realised a lot later when I could see they did not want to be in my life at all.

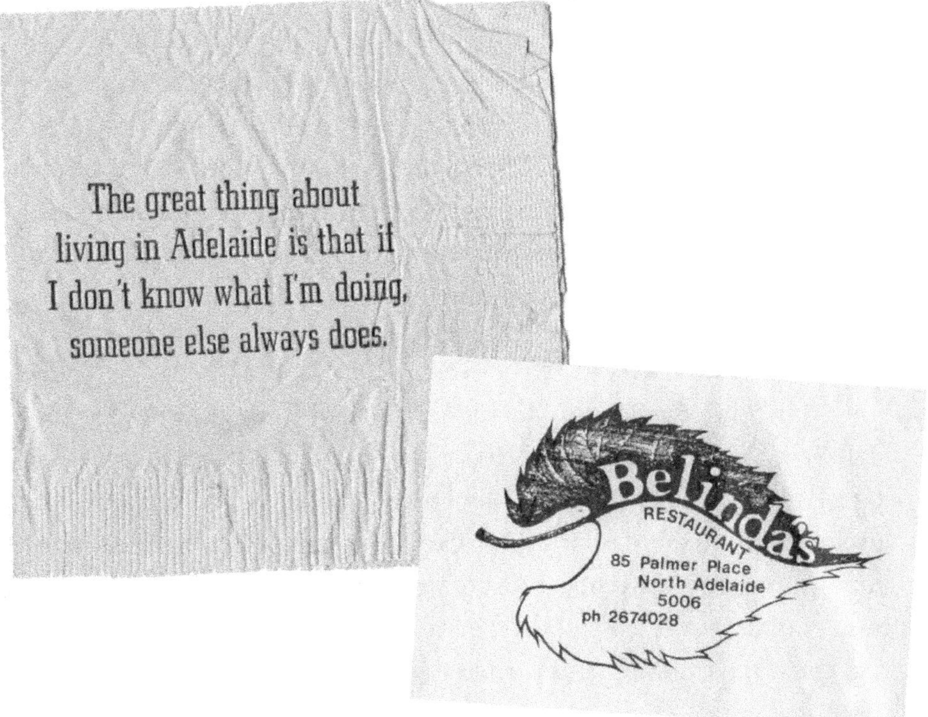

TOP HATS, BOW TIES, UNDERPANTS, SMELLY SOX

Somehow, while I was busy running Belinda's, I still managed a private life of my own. It was a little life tucked away in and around my professional life, away from the stresses that accompanied the hospitality business and out of sight of my children. Gone was the rich and famous centre stage at Robe Terrace. Gone were the Inner and Outer Mates created by the choices my parents made. Gone was the husband. Now it was all about my choices and me. And in my new world, I designed Top Hats, Bow Ties, Underpants and Smelly Sox.

Top Hats were driven to expand the creative mind. Bow Ties were the workers and artisans, very good listeners and communicators, and connected to the earth. Underpants were the sexual, sensual, lustful beings. Smelly Sox were none of the above. They were users, abusers, and predators, and appear later in my narrative.

MM was a Top Hat, Bow Tie and Underpants, but he had become a misty memory since my return to Adelaide. It was not his life to stay in town, and I had been banished from Kangaroo Island, so there was little hope for reconnection. The only wonderful remnant of the MM time is that my children and I still see him quite often. He was the photographer at Nick's wedding on the island and my grandchildren go camping with him. He is much happier and better off in his Kangaroo Island world of echidnas and sharing life with his long-time partner.

THE MANGO AND MOËT MAN

For a start, the Mango and Moët Man fitted all three categories – Top Hat, Bow Tie and Underpants. His name did not indicate that he was upper crust. I named him the Mango and Moët Man because he was luscious like a mango, sparkly, top class in nature and, what was most important, a true romantic. I had never had this in my life before, only in my fantasies, which suddenly came alive! He came into my life as my landscape gardener and turned my garden into a fairyland with a forest and pond.

It was months of landscape renovation that gave me an opportunity to get to know him from the outside in. There were long talks over tea breaks with always so much to say. I was captivated with his sensitivity, warmth and understanding of my past terrible years. Months went by and he turned my little place into paradise. I could see we were heading into a more intimate, most likely physical direction. Since I had just recovered from my separation with Ian and MM, the insanity of getting involved with another married man made me question very deeply what was happening.

He assured me that he and his wife had an open marriage, and indicated that she had someone else anyway, and that it would not affect their lives. Wisdom should have told me differently.

So, I had a secret affair in my upstairs room. It became our new venue for bed picnics, poems in my letterbox and phone calls to spur me on through the night-time business, which could go on until 2.00 am. At times, I heard stones at my window in the middle of the night. This was my year of romantic encounters, passion, hope and expressions of love. Time seemed to stand still. There seemed no end to our beginning.

But alas, the end came on Kangaroo Island where he came when I had a week off from the restaurant. Our ease and togetherness made him forget his other life. He didn't tell his wife when he was returning, and she decided 'it' had all gone too far. I had possessed him, and he had changed toward her. She made an ultimatum: we were never to see each other again. Moët' s fear and confusion tempered his thinking and my friend, lover, brother was drifting away from me. I could see it happening, but could do nothing to save him, them or us.

Just at the right time, a trip to Italy transported me into a different world with different thoughts. I felt peace for the first time in months. Still, the memories of Moët will never die. He still glistens in my mind, and there is something of him with me all these years later.

PERUGIA

When I departed for Perugia, Italy, I had no expectations or feelings of excitement. The winding down of Belinda's and long talks with Moët the day before departure left me with little feeling of anticipation. The thought of going to Italy with a group of Australians was off-putting if anything, but it was a special offer from the premier of the day, Don Dunstan, of five weeks' accommodation and an Italian course at the University of Perugia to promote language. It cost $4000. Luckily, my old partner in the dinner party scene, Judy Hardy, organised and participated in the whole trip. How could I resist?

The tedium of endless hours of flying was only broken by the change of crew at each stop. I had a prime viewing spot outside the galley. The Italian male stewards preened and swaggered down the aisles, the hostesses doing most of the work. They were the most extreme examples of egocentric people you could meet, but they kept me very entertained. I noticed that the customers got powdered milk and the stewards and hostesses got fresh milk, which they took home in their huge overnight bags. I always wondered what else they kept in there.

Covering my Australian suntan, I struggled into warm clothes and, feeling very much worn and dreary, waited for the bus that would carry us to Perugia. It came hours late, typical of the relaxed attitude that gives the Italian lifestyle its character. Four hours after that, we arrived in the city of Perugia. The tourists were divided into three sorts of accommodation – new, old and out of town. I picked old and fortunately only twelve Australians came with me. The rest were disposed of in two dreadful pensiones that had been over-booked. There were more problems and delays.

Pensione Todini, where I stayed, accommodated up to forty people, mainly students. As luck would have it, I acquired the only room to myself on the top floor. I also had a bathroom that I was fascinated to find had a toilet paper roll fixed under the shower. That was all I noticed. I was so exhausted, I fell asleep and woke up twelve hours later to a new day and a new adventure. At breakfast I met Mama Todini, a delightful middle-aged lady who ran the place with her son, Tomasis. I was not introduced to the other tables of locals, but taking a good look at them, I noticed they were mostly Italian students.

Orientation at the university was the morning's mission. We walked from the Todini along old cobblestone streets to the university. We entered an unbelievable building – a palace, with huge domed halls, a marble staircase and thousands of students of every colour and country gathered at the doors. My classroom was magnificent. It had gilt mirrors and frescos, old pews and ornate lights. It made me think going back to school could be fun. It was not fun. The lessons were three hours a day: exhausting, fast and difficult. The professor did not speak to us in English at all. Back came the old fears of being uneducated and dumb.

However, the magic of Italy started seeping into my bones on that first day. It generated a warmth and excitement in me I could not believe. With its dilapidated appearance, Perugia was wonderful. The atmosphere walking along Corso Venuti that evening was electric. People were everywhere and there were no cars. Laughter and eyes turned to look my way constantly and this fed my faded ego and fired my sense of involvement and importance. For the first week, every day after lessons, I went back to the pensione to study while the others went shopping. If I was to get involved totally in this environment, I wanted to be able to communicate as soon as possible. After lunch I had a siesta and another hour of study in the dining room. I hoped that by working in the dining room I might get some help from the locals. Tomasis often came to my rescue, but as he could not speak English it was difficult. I was still very dependent on our nightly Australian group communication, which became a ritual of drinks in someone's room before dinner – cheap wine and cheese, a walk around the shops or a concert or art show at night.

By the second week I was getting a little tired of Gladys with her mountainous bowls of bran, Jack's never-ending complaints about our tour organisation and Harry's glass eye, which dropped into his spaghetti when he got drunk. Added to this, Judy was travelling with a complicated Russian boyfriend and they didn't know where they stood with each other. I didn't know where I fitted in either. I was keen to extract myself from this Australian camaraderie now I was on the other side of the world. My problem was, how was I going to integrate into the new culture?

So far I'd had little contact with the other tables, until one evening a more able English-speaking man came over and introduced himself as Josue. He was about nineteen, of slight build, dark curly hair and a beautiful smile. He was from South America, studying Italian so that he could begin studying architecture the next year. That evening I went out with his friends – Franco, Jean Carlos, and Roberto, none of whom could speak English. This was my first chance to experiment with my Italian. Josue helped me out when I got really stuck, and they all enjoyed my attempts and encouraged me to say more. When I gave up in despair, I'd sit and listen to their conversation, trying to understand and not get frustrated at being shut off from my need for words. Night walks and coffee became an evening event.

Later that week I had a conversation with Josue about my 'sister', Figalinda, who I said had come to Italy as well. I explained that I had not introduced her to anyone, as she was outrageous and inclined to take over. Josue asked me to send her down that night so he could meet '*sorella*'. To oblige I began the creation of a new person. I straightened my hair and tied it up, painted my face, put on a new crazy long coat of patchwork, split to the waist, and black stockings, high-heeled boots and lots of jewellery. I appeared at the door of the dining room as everyone sat down for dinner. There was a stunned silence. Josue was delighted, and jumped to his feet to invite me to sit at their table. It was a fun, relaxing dinner. All the effort was worth it.

After we had eaten, the four boys whisked me off to a nearby disco called the Black Box. No one other than Josue could speak English, so I talked to him and danced with Jean Carlos well into the early morning. It reminded me of the time way back in Firenze when I had to choose between the three soldier boys. The only difference that time was that none of them could speak English. This time I had Josue on board but he didn't dance, so it was a curious three-way interaction. And something I did not complain about!

Josue was wise beyond his years, and his gift of speaking four languages fluently gave me a chance to plug into someone without language barriers. We met every afternoon after studies and talked for hours about his life, philosophy, dreams, aspirations and what my life was like back in Australia. Afternoons turned into evenings, expanding our creative minds as far as they could go, with me sucking in the vibrancy of my most favourite country on earth. Five weeks just slipped away.

After my Australian travelling companions had all departed I had three extra nights on my own with Josue. We started the first night at a bar and then went to dinner, followed by hot rum on the way home. It was a freezing night with continual drizzling rain and deserted streets, so when Josue suggested we buy some spumante and take it to the end of the Corso, I thought he was mad! There was a dry bench under a tree. We proceeded to drink the wine and sing to each other. He sang some of his Venezuelan songs and I sang some of mine. It was the most beautiful evening, with the rain falling against the lights of Perugia, and in that moment, Josue put his arms around me and kissed me as if I was the only person left in this world. All the conversations and thoughts were lost time. There was nothing left to do but run home soaking wet, up to my room, extract ourselves from dripping clothes and fall into bed. My mood of elation was met with total impotence on his part. I did not care but I cared for him. Spumante had numbed my apprehension.

Josue quietly crept away the next morning, while I lay thinking of the whole amazing experience. Josue's attitude to me, despite sexual inability, had been confusing. He seemed curious, innocent, passionate and shy. Had he had any past experience? It was not until I saw him at lunch that I had a chance to speak with him. He looked strained and pale. His lovely smiles a conflict to the sadness in his eyes. I asked him if he wanted to cancel that evening's arrangements and he said he didn't, so we met late afternoon at the Tit Bit Bar. There was something wrong. I made a last attempt to find out. Was it something I said? Or something I did? Or was it my age? The answer was no to everything. All I could manage from him was a comment that there was something he could not talk about and he felt that if he did, I would never want to speak to him again.

We went off to dinner, and although I could see it was still on his mind, we had a wonderful evening. On returning to the Todini, he asked if he could stay with me again. I was very careful to keep any pressure off him. There was a strange air about him. His awesome eyes burnt straight through me and I had a feeling that I had never experienced before or again. Making love was unimportant.

It was my last morning in Perugia, and my last attempt at trying to make Josue open up. I was unsuccessful. He left me with the promise of a letter, which arrived one week later and explained all of his hesitations: Josue had never been with a woman, and had for a long time considered himself homosexual, though he was uncomfortable with the label. Meeting me would put him on the path to a better understanding of what it means to be bisexual.

The end of my time in Italy was not the end of my connection with Josue. It was just the beginning. A year after Perugia, I travelled to Canada for his graduation and then we did New York. The following year he came to visit me in Australia. Since then, our correspondence has never ceased and a chance to meet up again is still an option. With culture, age and distance against us, our connection is extraordinary.

It has nothing to do with being male or female, or sexual orientation. It is a constant reminder to me that there is so much more to life than what I see or hear.

BOYS WITH UNDERPANTS

He came to paint my stairwell. He was very much younger than me, sexy and available. Painting the stairwell did not take long enough to get to know him, so I asked if he might paint everything. And he did. Last but not least my bedroom, and it was at the completion of that job that I realised he was very definitely Mr Underpants. What fun we had. It was an uncomplicated sexual adventure with no strings attached. My kids loved him and that was a must if he was to integrate into my life. He told them scary stories and we spent time on Kangaroo Island, and I rode on the back of his motorbike to places like Robe. Sometimes he helped out on the nights I ran Belinda's. I smoked a bit of dope with him, loved the sensual vibes we created and the zonked-out music. There was no bullshit and that's why I called him Trevvy True (TT). He was an interloper – here one minute, gone the next for weeks or months.

Eventually he returned to Perth to complete a course in interior design, and it was soon after he left that my periods stopped. Since I'd had a tubal ligation, I did not take much notice, and doctors reassured me it would be one in a million if I were pregnant. Four months later, an examination proved I was one in a million. I had an urgent abortion and my tubes were re-sealed. I didn't tell TT until thirty years later when we met up again. He was still Underpants when I met him years later. Thank goodness, I chose not to take up where I left off. Well, I did not take them off . . . maybe I have more wisdom than I thought?

Not long afterwards, a new lover came into my life as a Top Hat. He left over a year later as both Smelly Underpants and Socks. Clever, charismatic and handsome, he was an attractive package. He swept me off my feet. He moved in and sold my car. I gave up my business almost immediately, as it didn't work with another person living in my home. However, it was not the issues of being out of a job or having no car that sealed our fate. It was a dark aspect of him that grew out of a connection he had with someone else. It put my children's safety at risk and made me give him the ultimatum to leave.

This episode in my life could have taken chapters but I choose not to give it that amount of significance. What did I get from this experience? A chance to move on, to return my restaurant into a family home and get a job elsewhere. Guess who came back to my aid? Ron Tremaine, Top Hat and Bow Tie but, thank goodness, no further down. He offered me a top position in the running of the bistro connected to historic Ayers House on North Terrace called Paxtons. Before that, I was to join my best mate Primo Caon, owner of my favourite restaurant, on a culinary safari around France and Italy. It was a specialised pre-Ayers House food and wine fact-finding exercise, though Primo did not come in the end. Whom did I invite? My mother.

TRAINS TO NOWHERE

I decided to take my mother with me because she had been such a wonderful support at Palmer Place and I knew she would get a thrill revisiting her favourite countries. The plan of where to go was decided by the wine company, as they had all the contacts. The how was veiled in complete misunderstanding as they thought we had a car and didn't realise we were travelling by train. No one in their right mind would attempt to visit the far reaches of France by train. Some of our destinations were not even connected to a proper railway station.

It all began in Paris. My mother and I arrived at a tiny hotel on the Left Bank. The names and places are hazy now but I can still remember the main points. We had been given the addresses of four top establishments, including that of Paul Bocuse, and all of them proved to be very disappointing. Not the locations, decor or service, but the food. The food was an average version of my mother's French cooking back home, where we were brought up on béarnaise sauce, crepes and quenelles. Mum's traditional perfection all started with a little book she gave all her daughters *Oh, for a French Wife!*. We tried little cafés, which were far better value for money, but full of tourists. I had learnt from past experience that one should find where the locals eat to get the genuine deal, so we spent hours looking for evidence, which was revealed one night when we saw a long queue gather outside a place in the heart of Paris. After what seemed hours, we eventually got to sit down and the restaurant turned out to be Lebanese.

It was time to get going. The trip took us from Paris to Reims, Dijon, Nancy, Strasbourg and Lyon through the burgundy and champagne country, starting with a private lunch at Veuve Clicquot with Count Louis Dacourt in his chateau on the grounds. After that, there was an onslaught of private dinners with winery owners and we received red carpet treatment all the way. The wines were sensational, though I was thankful to be with my mother as we were in the company of all men. She learnt when I tugged on her skirt that I did not want to stay behind for a tete-a-tete.

The train experience on the other hand was a nightmare. We were now looking for the little town of Tain-l'Hermitage. My poor mother was being dragged on or pushed off trains that hardly stopped at the stations. Where were the stations? Not being able to speak French, we had no idea where to get off, as the larger towns disappeared behind us. It was a stroke of luck we found Tain-l'Hermitage. My mother and I didn't have seats so we sat on our suitcases. A sudden impulse that we were near Tain-l'Hermitage made me yank my mother from her suitcase and push her out the door into a paddock with a cobbled stone path leading both ways and no one in sight! We took a stab at going in the same direction as the train and after trundling our suitcases for about an hour, in the distance we saw a steeple and a tiny town nestled in the vine-covered hills. Relieved and elated, we continued to our destination with our hotel hopefully awaiting us.

The second stage of our train trip from France to Venice was even worse. After hours at the Paris railway station, we set off very wearily, settling in for a long night trip. We were ready to down our tonic for stress relief – Mogadon and neat brandy out of the cap. One hour out of Paris, I went to ask how long the journey was, only to be told the train was going to Zurich. They had dropped the carriages off at the back, where we were meant to be sitting. In shock, we fell out of the train at the border. It was the middle of the night. I ran from platform to platform trying to find someone who could speak English. They chose not to, even if they could. Somehow we arrived at the right platform. We finally boarded the correct train, though I was still wondering if we were off to Auschwitz. It was a dirty, third-class train with planks for seats and no evidence of safety or comfort. I suggested my mother lie down and use her handbag as a pillow to keep it safe from thieves (which I had been warned of). Many hours later with not one minute of sleep we arrived in Venice. Thank the Lord.

We had a couple of days to recover in a beautiful little hotel on the edge of the Grand Canal, opposite the island that was the home of the Hotel Cipriani. It was here I had an invitation to spend time in the kitchens of both Cipriani and Harry's Bar, two of the most prestigious restaurants in Italy at that time. We both loved the Venetian experience in every way. In those days, in the 1980s, tourism was not so bad, and it was off-season and beautiful autumn weather. The food, the ambience and the Italian magic gave me the feeling that I had come home.

It was lucky my mother was happy to sit on the Corso every day watching the passing parade. I was picked up every day by private motorboat and delivered across the water to the huge kitchen located under the hotel. This time I was lucky enough to speak and understand Italian. At the start I just soaked up the atmosphere of kitchen dynamics. It really inspired me. It was not the menu that was so special; it was really the systems that held the food and dining production together.

The maître d' was a powerful force between the kitchen and front of house. He had his eye on the ball at every moment. Different aspects of production were managed in stations and what I loved most was the camaraderie. The top chefs were delightful. I learned so much, and some of the things I used later when I set up my own restaurant, Jolley's Boathouse. For example, I employed more staff, I paid attention to details and I copied the system that allowed the staff a proper lunch break. A cloth was put over the central prep table and a bowl of pasta was the fuel that inspired top performances right until the end of shifts. In Australia I have not witnessed this. I realise it is about chasing the dollar, but that is often self-defeating, in that lack of nourishment means low energy levels for staff. Coffee fixes and after-shift liquor are not necessarily conducive to top performances the next day.

Looking back, my time in Italy gave me the best appreciation of all aspects of food, hospitality and culture. Italians seem to have an innate passion for their work and play and a true love of their country.

There was one other personally significant change during this trip away: my relationship with my mother. She was gutsy, funny, and courageous, now out from under my father's influence. She never complained, even with her eyes 'wide shut'. She fitted in and followed me around with ease, sometimes in situations that were really scary, showing me for the first time what she was really made of. Talk about the phoenix rising from the ashes!

I came back inspired for my new position at Paxtons. I completely redesigned the buffet, introduced a real antipasto table and trained new staff, except for the wonderful Sadie, a Lebanese woman who had been there since Ayers House started. It was my first experience of being employed in a professional kitchen and – what an eye opener. Although I was only in charge of the bistro side of the business, I was privy to the running of the fine dining section, as some aspects interlocked. This is where things fell apart. It was nothing like the kitchens in Europe. I found the ethics and practices abhorrent. In conflict with the head chef of the time, I resigned.

JOLLEY'S BOATHOUSE BISTRO

As I was standing with my mother above the old Jolley's Boathouse on the banks of the River Torrens in Adelaide, I had the same strange feeling I'd had thirty years before on the hills above Snelling Beach on Kangaroo Island. This time I thought, 'I want to turn this old place into a bistro.' Six months later I did.

I loved that it was a big, old historic building, five minutes from the centre of Adelaide, with the River Torrens passing right in front of its brick-paved entrance. In the past six years, I had achieved a certain amount of confidence and knowledge through the diversity of my culinary experiences. But I still felt I needed to get my teeth into something with substance. My mother, who was standing beside me, supported the idea, to at least find out who owned the building, to see if there was any chance of following the vision through. I researched and discovered it was owned by the Adelaide City Council and leased by the Altman family, who had run the paddleboats and kiosk for the past fifteen years.

I decided that I would make an appointment to meet with Keith Altman. Unknown to me, many potential restaurant owners had approached him to access his lease and develop the site, but he had turned them all down because their visions did not include running the kiosk, which he needed for his paddleboat customers. I came from a different perspective. I was a single, divorced woman with two young children and was willing to work the kiosk on weekends and public holidays. Keith talked about 'key money', goodwill and council rates, suggesting I make an appointment with the Adelaide City Council, which I did.

There was one year left of a five-year lease, with no right of renewal. My accountant said, 'No!' I changed my accountant and went back to Keith to establish the next move and also to learn about strategic negotiation. A few months later I had secured two deals. One was with the Adelaide City Council for a new lease (ten plus ten years with the

Jolley's Boathouse

right of renewal). The other deal was with the Altmans, who agreed to take in 'goodwill' and 'key money' which I think was in the vicinity of $60,000. Of course I didn't have that amount of money, but in came Louie, who had got me through so many difficult issues in the past. She suggested I ask my mother for a loan. My mother was very supportive of the proposition, as she knew she would have a secure job working with me just as she had at Palmer Place. She had really missed our culinary connection since I had closed down. As it turned out, I was able to pay her back, with interest, within the next two years.

Now I had secured the building, shock and fear took over. I had no idea how to put this together. There was just Mum and me, my children and Barb Cilento, who had helped me at Palmer Place and who was very willing to join in.

First it was necessary to attack the building as a whole. Apart from the position, the building really was a dump. Walls, which seemed to be made of cardboard, were infested with rats. Inside was a dark and dreary interior, comprising one front room and a counter for kiosk customers. There was barely a kitchen. Upstairs was another front room, balcony, one toilet and a storeroom, all in dreadful condition. A shed that opened onto the riverbank was not currently in use. In the old days this shed was used for regattas.

Where to start? Word got around very quickly of our new venture and in the process an acquaintance, a young married woman who I knew was a great cook, offered her services to help out. It was just what I needed. Janet was enthusiastic, hardworking and had the same bistro vision as I did. She also had access to some cheap alternatives. I had practically no budget to help get to stage one.

A monastery had burned down in the hills, leaving a kitchen full of commercial equipment. It had everything we needed, from stainless steel benches to pots and pans. We needed to get money for the renovations and we started by upgrading the kitchen, bar and front room, which would allow us to open up to a maximum of thirty patrons. We painted the walls a salmon pink, replaced the spew-coloured carpet with a rusty-coloured one, covered the tables with really thick plastic printed fabric and adorned the walls with blown up sepia photos of the Torrens in the old days. Of course we also put in the 'must have' greenery of ficus and ferns.

The kiosk moved next door into the boat shed. Here my sister Jill painted bright and cheerful murals of the rotunda at Elder Park on the walls and painted the concrete floor green. Next we relocated all the equipment we'd inherited in the lease, namely the soft serve, donut machines and numerous refrigerators, to that space. Nick and Rachel were ready and keen to run the kiosk on weekends and public holidays, thinking it would be a pleasant respite from school.

On the bistro side, there were Janet Vincent and me in the kitchen, with Ma and Barb Cilento out in front. It started not quite as a bistro but more like a self-service bar. There was a chalkboard of specials and everything else was set up behind the food bar with Janet and me in charge of serving the hot food. Self-serve was salad and sweets. We had immediate clientele from the old Palmer Place days, and from even

Old Jolley's

earlier than that. A middle-aged gentleman came up to the bar and told me he had been to my Roman feast back at Robe Terrace and I had put his underpants in the freezer. He must have been wearing a toga!

It was not long before we were full every day for lunch, and we soon realised we had to start renovations on the outside brick patio that extended almost out to the river edge. This was achieved by building a pergola with a clear plastic roof, plastic roll-down blinds and, over that, roller doors to secure the whole area at night.

There were awnings to camouflage the doors, and bright yellow umbrellas with tables all along the riverfront, which gave the European alfresco feeling I loved so much. My vision was to follow another Italian tradition – to create a family business that would employ family, children and friends – though this was challenged in every single way.

When the outside bistro really started, gone was the old formal à la carte. Instead we introduced handwritten menus, changing weekly, and more staff. The menus were a challenge. I couldn't spell. My writing was disgraceful. To cover my mistakes I created a new persona to overcome my dyslexia and learned to write beautifully in a whole different style.

We designed a menu with one price for any two courses. This was not a place of quick turnover. Most of our clientele stayed for hours. It was in such a wonderful position and our front-of-house was able to entice everyone into pre-lunch cocktails, sweets, coffee and liqueur.

Barb was a gem – fun, eccentric and colourful. Everyone loved her. She had a huge social base with many women friends and was a loyal trusted core of the front-of-house team. My mother and Barb were followed by Suzie and Lynn, personally recommended professionals, both very attractive, great at seducing the men to drink up and attending to them until they fell out of the door at 6 pm. They were a stunning bunch.

Meantime, back in the kitchen things were moving pretty fast. At thirteen and sixteen, Rachel and Nick also needed extra staff to support the influx of river traffic. Not being very successful at school, they found the kiosk a refreshing weekend diversion, filled with many very funny moments. Nick's big daily responsibility was to empty the soft serve machine, which involved dismantling and washing about eight parts and dozens of washers and valves. One morning, I came in early to open up and reaching into the dark for the switch, I stepped onto the concrete floor only to slide. I was skating over a sea of white sticky 'goo' – one washer put on back to front meant the machine had pumped the whole mix of soft serve onto the floor!

The fun side of Nick came out when he took the leftover bucket of soft serve mix at the end of each day down to the river bank and gave out spoons and free scoops to all the down-and-out kids running amok down there.

Rachel was put in charge of the bicycle-driven ice-cream cart. She would ride along the river selling ice-cream, usually cheap because she could not add up. She made even less when kids stole all the ice-creams from her. I took her very quickly off that job and put her back into the kiosk where she excelled.

STRANGE ENCOUNTERS OF FOUR KINDS

Rachel and Nick ended up befriending all the down-and-outs and strays along the river. One particular homeless man comes to mind. He slept in the park. He was a gentleman of European background, and had huge issues to do with the Second World War. The first time he came into the kiosk, out of his huge dirty army coat came a little wet leather pouch full of grass and one-dollar notes. Every time he came, he asked for a 'honeymoon sandwich' (honey and white bread), would only pay in wet one-dollar notes and would never accept any change. Rachel put up a little clothes line to hang out his dollar notes until they dried. They welcomed him and listened to his stories, and I was so proud of my children's compassion and patience.

Nick's other job was to load up the two soft drink fridges from the back, their fronts facing into the kiosk. One day as he was loading the drinks, a little girl approached the fridge to get one. As she opened the door, Nick's voice filtered through the cans, 'Hello little girl. I am your talking fridge. What would you like to drink?' 'Coke please,' she answered. With that, a huge hand (Nick was fifteen and nearly six feet tall) appeared and delivered the Coke to her. The look on her face was magical. Nick repeated this fun game any moment he had the time.

Then there was the army barracks, just around the corner from Jolley's. At certain times, with no warning, the whole army appeared, all wanting hot pies and pasties. There was usually only Rachel and her cousin Georgina to serve them. What a nightmare! There would be hot, warm, cold, frozen pies and pasties all rotating in the heating facilities. Even though the end results were often far from perfect, the army always went out of the door happy and grateful for the effort and style of the girls.

I have no idea how I got to employ staff with disabilities. Maybe my experience at sixteen at the Woodville Spastic Centre inspired me. Gail was both physically and emotionally impaired, which taught the rest of the team to respect and encourage people like Gail and Tony.

The Jolley's employment experience was not unlike that of Jamie Oliver years later, and was very comfortable and familiar to me in so many areas – a collective team of young teens, between fourteen and eighteen, who made up the labour machine of kitchen and kiosk. The only staff with experience were front of house and office. No one was acquired through advertising. All were word-of-mouth. Louie, my loyal supporter and mentor, started the ball rolling. She knew me better than anyone. She knew my shortcomings and my abilities, so I trusted her suggestions and directions. She had a daughter Meim, fifteen and just out of school, in desperate need of a job.

I trialled Meim for two weeks. She was exceptional – feisty, hard-working and keen, a real gem. I employed her in the kitchen doing dishes and two years down the track she was number one in the kitchen. She stayed till the very end and married my only Regency Park apprentice, chef Phil.

Then Louie introduced me to Tony. He was from a severely dysfunctional family, in his thirties, scared, illiterate and non-communicative. He started as yard man and was responsible for the collection of rubbish and shed clean-up. Two years later, he had advanced to wine store, for which he had to learn to read and write. He was then dishwasher, kitchenhand and finally in his whites in the kitchen cooking with me. He went on after Jolley's changed hands to an important position in a city hotel kitchen.

I could go on and on, but Donna, for example, was exceptional. As the team grew, so did the business – six days plus three nights a week. My mother and I could see we had taken on a huge responsibility, a job we did not take lightly. Work was a hundred per cent focused but, when it was playtime, we also gave a hundred per cent to the fun and games. I had strict policies about honesty, waste, stocktakes and training programs that required me to be in the kitchen 7.30 am until 5.00 pm, training the staff in my special style of cuisine.

I expected results but I also gave the staff considerations that most

Selection of Two Courses minimum $17.00
Dessert from blackboard extra
$2.00 Surcharge Sundays & public Holidays

~ Menu ~

~ Soup of the Day ~

Buckwheat Blini trio:
Selection of smoked salmon, sour cream raw onion & egg, cucumber & mint with hot blinis.

Thai Seafood Salad Antipasta.

Tomato cups filled with fresh basil & motzerella & artichoke on bed of bacon & spinach.

~ Pasta of the Day ~

Smoked Chicken & Duck Terrine with pink peppercorns Port, orange & ginger Sauce.

~ Prawn, Herb & Vermouth Omelette ~

Whiting Veronique with grapes & light creamy sauce

Cold Trout stuffed with Julienne of Vegetables and New Orleans Sauce

Cold fillet of Beef with carpaccio Sauce (Rare)

~ Catch of the Week ~

From the Charcoal

Marinated Skewers of chicken & almonds, aromatic & spicy on bed of Basmati & Wild Rice

Porterhouse with whole mustardseed, Horseradish & Sorrel.

Noisettes of lamb with mint glaze.

restaurants, except those in Europe, would never entertain. The staff could cook their own lunches at eleven before lunch set up, they could take home leftovers, and they joined in the wine tasting and fun and games we had after work. We made Christmas and birthdays a huge 'family' affair. I felt I had adopted these young people, since most of them came from broken homes and difficult circumstances. I became Smummy (substitute mummy), and my mother was known as Bundy (the name her grandchildren called her).

Unfortunately, Nick and Rachel had a difficult time with me, because I expected them to set an example and I did not want to give them special treatment. It made my role as both their mother and boss almost impossible. This will be elaborated on later.

Presentation was a huge thing. I had the most beautiful herb and flower suppliers. I could create plate ideas never seen before – borage flowers, chilli flowers, zucchini and carrot ribbons, oiled lemon leaves and the usual special effects of tomato and radish roses. The flamboyance of the sweets was our specialty – pinnacles of spun toffee, chocolate butterflies, wild colours, edible flowers and lots of piped cream, layer upon layer of deliciousness. How did we get into this and who executed the resulting works of art? It was Emma and Rachel's rise in the sweet department. Emma was a naughty little girl of fifteen, untamed by a mother who was desperate to find her daughter employment. What impressed me was that Emma's mum was a professional chef and food stylist and had taught Emma everything. She was obviously a talented and creative girl. I took her on straight away. Rachel, keen to move out of the kiosk and spread her creative wings, joined Emma in the kitchen. Emma later became top of her profession in Australia. Rachel also did well and became known as the Queen of Fantasy Desserts. She has cooked in restaurants all over the world.

On a very positive note, our pairing of food and wine was ground-breaking. We had my old friend Primo as consultant for our wine list, and my careful menu plan featured innovative, multicultural dishes, always one step ahead of the trend. I had arrived on the scene of nouvelle cuisine – simple, minimalist, French-inspired. I rebelled and set up a food concept that was fun, creative and diverse. The main menu was made up of 'food of the world', food for vegetarians, and food for meat-eating men who loved chargrill, with sweets that were extravagant and over the top. In one memorable example, when Mick Jagger came for lunch Rachel created our special 'forbidden fruit' with huge chocolate lips on top!

Around this time I also requested to take on an apprentice from Regency Park. It was unusual, because they normally only placed their students with qualified trained chefs, which I was not. Fortunately, they could see that my years of experience, based on what I had learnt largely from my mother, was good enough. So in came Philip. Philip, like all my staff, on first meeting seemed very quiet, scared and young. I was also scared, terrified of being his mentor and teacher. The beauty of Philip was, with his Regency Park training, he was a true professional, dedicated to excellence from the word go. He never lost his cool, did whatever was expected of him and he never turned into a lunatic like the rest of us when we were unleashed. In retrospect, I think Philip found the environment at Jolley's rather disturbing, but it did not stop him from marrying Meim, and both of them went on to top executive positions in hotels and catering.

The dynamics of Jolley's were extraordinary and unique. Another dimension was added when I took on extra staff from very well-off families. They had all the opportunities available to them, but no drive or incentive. Much like me, they too had not been successful in their education. These different characters caused some difficult situations when they went haywire – class distinctions, competition and resentments. It took huge personal input from both my mother and me and we gave them extra consideration, understanding and control to maintain harmony. There were many tearful and revealing talks in our office.

On the other hand the celebrations, achievements and positive outcomes far outweighed the negative. I can only think of two of my staff who left voluntarily. Prior to these challenges and successes, I had tried to employ my extended family as they do in European family businesses. It was one of my initial disappointments to find this was very difficult to make work in the excitement and challenge of getting Jolley's Boathouse up and running.

Meanwhile, back in the bistro, we were well on the way. Unfortunately my right hand chef, Janet, decided to leave because of the change to à la carte, which she found too stressful. She loved it best when it was just me and her in the kitchen. Sadly, she passed away suddenly several years later and I most probably didn't show her how much I appreciated her part in the launch of the Jolley's experiment.

In relation to stress, what about me? I was catapulted into a situation I had never experienced. Financial loans, profit and loss, wine appreciation, staff training, food outlets, weddings and special events, festivals, kiosk management etc. I had a 'nervous breakdown' every few weeks. These were often fixed by a stiff brandy (Dad's influence) in the office. Rosters went haywire, food ran out and sometimes it was far from perfect. There were many mistakes, and dramas daily. *Fawlty Towers* seemed a good description, with my inexperience in running the kitchen meaning I could not oversee every plate that went out. Luckily for me, the front of house was a very professional team who did a wonderful job. Lynn had style, sexy legs and lips. We called her 'Lynny Loo Lips'. She was very serious about her job, which was great. Suzie was petite and seductive, wowed the men, and was able to get them drinking our beautiful cocktails. Barb came with me from Belinda's restaurant. She was a colourful and extroverted character wearing flamboyant outfits, with flaming red hair. My mum was of course a winner. At the age of seventy, she was out in front charming everyone and also helping to patch up the mistakes.

We had some very funny moments when my children moved from

kiosk to the bistro. Nick, at seventeen, was keen to give front of house and the wine section a go. It was completely alien to him and he made mistakes only he could get away with. His manner and character made it possible for me to let him continue. For example, there was one time when he tipped orange juice down the back of a nun's habit, another when he dropped butter on a silk coat, and there were many spilt drinks and wrong orders. I gave enormous compensations – free meals, wine and dry cleaning. Even Rachel, summoned from the kiosk to serve tables when we were short-staffed, dropped a huge steak on a gentleman's lap and ran away in fright. What was extraordinary was that in almost every case our clientele were very tolerant and came back for more. Jane Reilly, a weather girl on television, loved Nick's style so much she requested he serve her table whenever she came to lunch. We were a fun group out front, a bit naughty and cheeky but always with the customer in mind.

SWINGING THE BÉARNAISE SAUCE

Joe was another young relative of Louie's, and he was very cheeky, creative and headstrong. He certainly needed some control, and a feeling of belonging. Sometimes he took things a little too far, just to get a reaction.

Joe would make bulk béarnaise sauce. We loved the traditional French favourite. It was always a winner – no short cuts here. During one lunchtime, in a silly mood, he decided to give the béarnaise sauce an Aussie twist and swung the sauce like a billycan of tea over his head. He had the hot buttery mix in a plastic bucket. As he swung it over his head, the handle flew off and the whole bucket landed upside down on top of the cappuccino machine, which was a huge, ornate and antique piece of equipment with silver filigree. It was about 11.30 am, just before lunch set up. I turned my head in shock to see litres of hot sauce slide down the sides of the machine onto the floor, splattering onto the walls, cups and surrounding people. Having learned from

Ayers House days not to confront embarrassed staff in front of others, I decided the best way out was to leave the kitchen. Luckily it was at the stage at Jolley's when the place could survive without my constant input. Lunch would go on, so, with staff sniggering in the kitchen and Joe hiding, I went home to simmer down. Later I was very relieved to have Joe come to my house and apologise for his antics. He is now a top chef in Melbourne.

ROTTWEILERS AND THE SECURITY MAN

The Jolley's Boathouse site was an icon – a famous old building on the River Torrens, behind an infamous old toilet block, which was a meeting place for gay men. The park around it was a sleeping place for the homeless, and the river hid murders and robberies. We were broken into twice in a couple of months before we took action. The building was impossible to secure since the back was just a series of tin sheds. I am not sure where we got the idea, but quite suddenly we had employed Frank, a middle-aged, eccentric security guard with two huge rottweilers.

They were all in residence every night from dusk till dawn. We only came in once he had left with his vicious hounds. He had a nightly journal and wrote in every detail of all the activities that went on around the building. I'm sure he was a voyeur. We had a very funny relationship with him. We left him treats and notes and he gave us much entertainment reading his journal – strangers in the night fornicating in the bushes, police raids and, on a much more disturbing note, drownings in the river and dead bodies. We felt completely protected with our new team guarding the premises – until years later, not long before I sold the business. Rachel came to work very early one morning to be confronted by two huge dogs that bounded up to her, wagging their tails, and licked her all over. So much for the vicious hounds.

looking
Falling
Bernaise
swinging the Bernaise

As was the norm for restaurants, we had regular visits to Jolley's by the health inspector. He was a delightful man who became my mother's best friend. We had huge logistic problems that came with the premises, mainly rats and a building that made it difficult to maintain our health standards. Control over produce was not the issue, but the building was very run-down. We had no spare income to upgrade more than the bare necessities, so we were very grateful to the health inspector for turning a blind eye to areas of the restaurant we could not fully fix. The tin sheds out the back and cracked concrete floors created a third-world environment. Mum would welcome the inspector through the doors like a long lost friend and they would sit down and have lunch, which meant he did not have much time to spend finding fault, and Mum had a break from hostessing. I think he was in love with her!

Jolley's staff loved the food fights along the riverbank – mistakes, leftovers, Milo and powdered milk were the usual favourites, but they also liked jellies, which were like rubber, and leftover soft serve. The tension among my young staff built up and dissipated. We all needed a release after a pressure cooker shift. Thanks to the wonderful bunch of wine merchants and owners, we had at least three wine tastings a week and we drank the dud ones after work. These were not late affairs, as we all had to work early the next day. The special events behind closed roller doors were the highlights – birthdays, farewells and any other excuse to celebrate. I was most proud of how my young staff really respected my generosity and put in one hundred per cent. Nothing was ever stolen, or taken for granted. Only when the business was sold and all the treats taken away by the new management did things start to disappear out the door.

TA TA JOLLEY'S

The end of Jolley's was a relief for me but a total shock for my mother. I had hoped I could keep my children employed there by selling the lease to my ex-husband, Ian, and his wife. It seemed a good idea at the time.

I was to be kept on as consultant with the staff still employed. As soon as handover occurred, it was very evident that there was no consideration and respect for me, and this extended to my staff, including the children. It became apparent that I was not wanted and I left. The staff and my children followed me soon after. I fled to Kangaroo Island to squat on my land in a fury where I wrote to Ian's new wife:

Dear Rose,
You have got my husband, you have got my business, but you can't have my Kangaroo Island house.

And what about my children? Where did they fit in? I think they were very happy to get on with their individual lives and away from me. Nick seemed pretty okay with life. He had a girlfriend. He was into his art and had his first exhibition in the shed down the bottom of our garden. Rachel was in the midst of a relationship with the unspeakable Peter. I was in shock, very upset, and blamed myself for not being around to protect her from such a crazy man. The only way I could see to change the direction of Rachel's life was to send her away overseas, on a culinary fact-finding mission.

The move out of Jolley's made me realise how grateful I was to the Outer Mates of that time. These were the young chefs of Adelaide who made such a difference to sourcing the sauce. We had held such dynamic meetings at Lucia's in the Central Market with Gabriel Gaté, Peter Jarmer, Nick Papazahariakis and co., swapping ideas and amalgamating food and friendship. And to Primo Caon, who was a great mentor and leader in the food and wine industry right up until 2010, I would like to say a personal thank you. (The Central Market on Fridays is still my favourite experience. To shop, to chat and finally to top it off with a gin cocktail at the Kangaroo Island produce stall – who could ask for anything more?)

Why did it end? What made me decide to abandon a really extraordinary and successful business venture in the middle of its success? It was pretty simple: I refused to let go of the cooking supervision with my young staff. I refused to get a team of experts to sort me out and become a 'professional'. It was really just too much for one person to run. My mother, on the other hand, was in her element. I was worn down, with the added pressure that comes with a certain amount of notoriety. There was no other life, just seven days a week of work.

And then there was Kennino.

KENNINO BARRUCHI

Lebanese, Irish, Kiwi, Catholic: what a mix! A cocktail I could never reproduce. It was not long after I set up Belinda's that I first met Kennino. I had a very good doctor friend who had bought the old church that faced into the bottom of my garden. Peter did not like living on his own, or cooking, so it was not such a surprise when one evening I saw someone upstairs, toiling over a hot stove in Peter's upstairs kitchen. Not long after that I met him when Peter was entertaining, and learnt that Ken had a live-in gay relationship back in Sydney that was not going so well, hence his visits to Adelaide.

Over the years, my friendship with Ken developed on his numerous trips to Adelaide. We went to the same parties and danced our feet off. At other times, he would join my mother for lunch at Jolley's while I was cooking. We kept up a very special connection for over ten years.

Kennino was a truly beautiful man with complexities and issues I understood. He was also a creative gourmet, a poet, and my soulmate. We were in sync on every level except sexually, which, in retrospect, came as a breath of fresh air. He gave me freedom of expression, no expectations, and a playmate around the edges of Jolley's. My personal life certainly changed when he moved in to live with me. Kennino's life in Sydney and the chaos of his relationship there had come to an end and there was a magic ingredient in our combination that seemed very appealing to both of us. Nick and Rachel loved him. He had such

For Kenny, 1980

You crazy mad creature
Hungry for living,
Lustful and sinful
But so good at giving,
You have given me pleasure
It's also a joy,
To scratch (just the surface)
Of such a nice boy.
You may not make millions,
Perspectives unclear,
And life may be tiresome,
Now that you can hear,
Confusion, delusion
I know it so well,
But it's not a bad lifestyle
It has a good smell.

There's so much to you
Kenny I like what I see,
Perhaps it's because
You're a lot quite like me,
If the world doesn't need us
We'll find a new place,
And go to the grave
With a smile on our face.
Ta ta for now Kenny
It's sad that you leave,
But I'm not going to suffer
I'm not going to grieve,
Accept the goodbyes
As I know for a fact,
Just like it's the theatre
It's not the last act!

Age: thirty-eight

humour, pathos, silence, madness and creativity at every level. My children were pretty young at the time and he always had time for them. They played stupid games, usually with food, like blowing Milo at each other, and on one special occasion Nick paid Kennino back for something by mixing cornflakes with gravy and tipping it over his head and watching it drip down into his ears. Kennino never moved a muscle and just kept on eating his dinner.

Six months passed and what happened next was a total shock. After he came back from the funeral of his dad in New Zealand, Kennino revealed his true nature. He talked about his sadness for missed opportunities, and his life on the road as a manager to a rock and roll band. He had a sudden desire to take life with both hands and make things happen before it was too late. Just like that, we plunged into what I thought was impossible and what I had never expected – an incredible love story and a sexual connection that just seemed like fate and destiny. He moved out of the little room at the back and into my bedroom. We had extravagant dinners, played the piano, wrote poetry and he painted the inside of the house a deep and beautiful rose colour. He planned events, a horse and carriage for my mother's birthday and a farewell for Emma, one of my staff. It was a progressive feast with candles out in my little garden spelling her name. On the wedding of Sarah Ferguson we had a lunch and he dressed as a bishop and I came as the bride.

Kangaroo Island became our playground as well. Here we dug out the river to meet the sea, had picnics in the hills, camped in tents and joined in with my children and their friends.

Everything changed overnight. Kennino came back from a check-up with his doctor to tell me he was HIV positive. The lifestyle he had taken on after the end of his marriage had been off the rails. He had taken drugs, drunk too much and been promiscuous. But the test result was a huge shock to both of us. It was not that we had not practised safe sex, or that we could not cope with new rules, it was the stigma and the fear of telling my children the probability he would die. But this did not change my attitude to him or my position in his life. In fact, I offered him a job to take over the kitchen from me to give me time out. I wanted him in my life as long as possible, but I did not expect a deep and consuming depression to creep into our time together.

Kennino's input at Jolley's was very difficult on both sides. My staff were used to 'Smummy' running the kitchen. They did not accept the change well. Kennino found it almost impossible to run a mob of strong-minded women who did not feel he had the expertise to take over. Maybe he didn't, but it seemed the only way out at the time. My feeling of freedom was outweighed by the obvious stress this move put on everyone else. I could not go back. I did not know how to go forward. The only solution was to sell, which I did.

Not long after this decision, Kennino decided to go back to Sydney for a week. Four days later, I received a phone call from his good friend to tell me Kennino had taken his life. His last tests had not been so good and he didn't want to be around my children or me. He died on 24 August 1987. The only consolation in the sadness of Kennino's death was that he did not have to suffer full-blown AIDS, and we did not have to suffer watching him die. He made that possible by returning to Sydney and I was grateful my children were not around. The lasting memory of Kennino was in his wonderful poem he wrote to me in the months before his death. It is one I will always cherish.

May 1987

Some souls may never unite in this man made world,
Yet after its penance will come a reward so great.
Let's not believe or hope as only despair results.
Ours is no mortal feeling, nobody can understand,
They do not see or even know the marriage of our spirit.

RUNNING AWAY

It was the year after I sold Jolley's, Kennino was gone, my children were living at Palmer Place, and my mother was without a job. I had left my very busy, successful life and friends back in Adelaide and gone to Kangaroo Island alone.

It's still something I am trying to control, my propensity to run away when things get difficult. I ran away to the chooks in fear of my father at Robe Terrace, I ran into the streets when upsets occurred in my marriage, and I arranged trips overseas to run away from everybody. Now I was running to Kangaroo Island to establish my half ownership of the Cliff House where Ian had been living for the past few years.

Louie had taken an important role in my healing process. I saw her often, and in one of those sessions she insisted I squat on the land to assert my right to my half share of Cliff House, as she thought I might lose it. This revelation was a shock. Kangaroo Island was my sanity, my spiritual home, and an intrinsic part of my life since I was born. Ian had remarried and his new wife did not get on with my children, which was even more reason to do something as soon as possible. I did not inform him of my plan to settle there. I simply said it was a little break for me now I was free from Jolley's. It was against my nature to do what Louie had suggested. The act of deception did not rest well with me. Fortunately, my mother had found herself a boyfriend and my children were still employed at Jolley's, where they were trying to make sense of all the new rules and dynamics they did not understand.

The rich life I had enjoyed in Adelaide with my mother suddenly imploded on my inner source, and that was an experience I did not want to face. I was totally on my own, just surrounded by nature. It was terrifying listening to the beat of my heart as I had no one to rely on, with nothing to do and nothing to say. I had made this rash decision and I was now stuck with it.

As I could see no way out, I had to embrace the experience with creative gusto and courage. I went on weird diets of brown rice and read every 'woo woo' book I could lay my hands on, although some turned out to be essential: those of Deepak Chopra and Shakti Gawain. Then I joined the Buddhist movement and helped to raise money for the new *stupa* being built just up the road from me. I studied the *Lam Rim* (slow journey), from cover to cover. Funny about that. I believed if I emptied out all the doing, the being would come naturally. But alas there were no blinding lights. Bridget, my pet magpie, saved my life that year on Kangaroo Island.

I had been terrified of magpies my whole life. They used to swoop at me on my way to school. In subsequent years, Nick found Bridget who had fallen out of her nest, and with the help of Mountain Man (who was still in our lives at the time) we learnt how to train her. For a start, she stayed safely in my wired vegetable garden, until I was able to let her inside to live with me. She slept on a branch in the living room and came up to my bed in the morning. Then she would lie under my chin, play with my hair and hang upside down on my fingers. I spent hours with her. Soon she was free to fly outside. I waited for her to disappear and never come back, but she didn't leave. She stayed the whole year, ruling the sky above the Cliff House but still sleeping at night inside with me. Bridget would sit on the beach with the seagulls. I would surprise tourists when I went down to get her. Whenever I sauntered past to where she sat, Bridget would hop on my hand, then I would lay her on her back, legs in the air, and put her on top of my Akubra hat and march past the surprised faces of those watching.

This was living, wild and free, at its very best, and my bird fascination really took off from that time on. I went on to protect wild birds – the glossy blacks – from feral cats. I trapped twenty in the first summer. I studied the little plovers that built their vulnerable nests on the open sand and I tried to control car access to the beach to protect them. There was an osprey (sea eagle) that flew over the house every day

Whirly Bird with Bridget

at the same time and ate the snapper on Nick's fishing line when he pulled them into the boat. Little blue wrens would come inside to visit. It was no wonder my nickname became Whirly Bird.

In the spring of 2016 Rachel connected to magpie magic herself. All the memories of Bridget came back to me, and I could experience with her the joy she was getting on a day-to-day basis from Queenie's antics, even more bizarre than Bridget's. I watched Queenie as she welcomed guests – some a little apprehensive – as they arrived at the opening of the Fig Tree where Rachel and Sasha had set up their restaurant.

'Wild and free' felt just like me, unencumbered by outside influences and peer group pressures; no expectations, deadlines or rules or regulations. That year on Kangaroo Island reconnected me to basics and replaced my chaotic inner life with creative thoughts and visualisations. I thought I had it made. I finally understood loneliness

Rachel with Queenie

and aloneness and have never felt either since. But to think I had all the answers was a dreadful mistake.

Suddenly I was catapulted back to the reality of life. Ian was aware of my extremely long stay and I became very concerned and shocked by what was happening back at Palmer Place where Nick and Rachel were left to fend for themselves. They ran riot. Actually, I think Nick loved the freedom. He had begun painting. Rachel, on the other hand, was far too young and without my supervision (however permissive that was) had even less structure to her life.

It was two phone calls that brought me back to reality. Nick rang one night traumatised by a book he had picked up dealing with the influences of sexual trauma (paedophilia). He was wondering if he was gay. I sent him up to see Louie who gave him the counselling she was so good at. The other phone call was from an artist, a friend of Nick's who had befriended Rachel. 'Psycho' rang me and said, 'Hello, Belinda. Just thought I'd tell you I am fucking your daughter.'

This became my worst nightmare. I was powerless to do anything about it. I believe that this experience really destroyed Rachel's adolescence, and that it was totally my fault. I returned to Adelaide and, in consultation with Ian, decided to take instant action and send Rachel overseas for a year, an idea that – thank God – she didn't reject. In fact, it was the best thing that could have happened.

Once Adelaide was settled, I went back to Kangaroo Island, where the source of my creativity lay. Creative thinking and outlets were a constant source of joy and fulfilment. I still did not need a partner or lover, nor did I need to blackmail my children into joining me as I had sorted them out. On Kangaroo Island I was able to shine like a star in my own right. Nothing was too difficult or complicated. Invigorated and inspired, I thundered through new projects. I accomplished in one day what might take weeks for others.

Eventually ownership of the Cliff House was mine, but at a price. Every penny went into buying Ian out. The unknown price I had to pay was squatting on the land and selling Jolley's.

My father had passed away. My mother's boyfriend had passed away as well. So up Mum popped, back into my life and back onto Kangaroo Island. Mum went back to live in the old homestead she and my father had purchased years before.

Her property consisted of 100 hectares of rural land, the homestead and two run-down dwellings, one fibro, the other a crumbling limestone ruin. After the Cliff House was given a makeover, Mum decided she would like to renovate the two cottages. I drove the creative aspect and we were a great team because we were both inspired by having a new project to get our teeth into. We completely rebuilt the stone cottage and the fibro got a patch up. But, as the Cliff House was rented out, I was already wondering where I would live.

I think I must have been a gypsy in a past life! Out of a local's

First business brochure for Cliff House

backyard rubbish dump, I extracted a bunch of old caravans, which I concealed in the trees not far from the Cliff House. I connected one caravan to power by means of a very long extension cord. I cut one caravan in half and attached it to a deck and made a mobile bathroom out of a tin base. I found another caravan in a pigsty. This became my residence for the next five years.

It was a creator's dream, a conservative's nightmare. I most probably loved it best out of all my nesting spots. I called it Marrakech, and filled it with old Afghan rugs and camel's necklaces I had acquired via barter at an Arab feast. This was the birth of not only Marrakech, but of the new Settlers' Cottage and Beach House, which had the huge advantage of facing north, right on the edge of beautiful Snellings Beach. Renting them was a breeze.

As soon as I feel depressed, bored or uninspired I build something. It started when I was a child. It was an obsessive exercise. I turned our nursery into a house within a house. I tipped furniture upside down, created dark cubby houserooms that Jill and I would crawl into and take food and torches there to play house. Then it expanded into the garden. I placed nests on top of bushes, on the roof, in the shed, in the chook yard, and really anywhere I could turn something into a secret hideaway.

Marrying Ian had been a perfect continuation of my passions as we moved from place to place, building and renovating, and I loved every moment – except the move to Glenelg where Eliza died. Kangaroo Island provided a creative palette for my mum and me with our continual makeovers of the old and obsession with building the new.

My biggest building project was Osprey, which allowed me to rent the Cliff House all year round. It was my environmental Top Hat era. I sold some of the land and built a rammed-earth wind-powered Moroccan-style dwelling all by myself.

I had a magnificent collection of Outer Mates and eccentrics who became my best friends in the process. These were the times when life was without effort or hardship, just pure unadulterated excitement and joy. Eventually I pulled down Marrakech and got approval to build a one-room manager's cottage, which became my next home. I called it Illuminare, which was an apt name. It is still there for me now.

CHAPTER 4

Sweets

Forbidden fruit

INGREDIENTS

4 egg whites
1 cup raw sugar
¼ cup chopped walnuts
¼ cup dried figs
½ tablespoon cornflour

METHOD

There is a bit of finesse to making meringues. In this recipe you need to be extra diligent due to the variation of raw sugar granules needing to be dissolved in the beating process. Egg whites must be room temperature and good quality. Check all equipment is grease free, and measure all of the ingredients prior to beginning.

Set beater to 7 or ¾ speed and add whites and beat until starting to firm.

Very slowly and steadily add the sugar, a handful at a time. Try to wait until the sugar has dissolved until adding more. The volume will increase as you add. If you do not add the sugar quickly enough, the meringues will dry out. The mixture should be silky.

Slow the beaters down to the lowest setting. Add all the remaining ingredients.

Quickly spoon out mixture onto baking paper in individual nests.

Cook in oven at 100°C for an hour.

Persimmon pudding

INGREDIENTS

1 cup sugar
1 cup flour
1 teaspoon carb soda
½ teaspoon salt
2 teaspoons cream of tartar
1 teaspoon cinnamon
¼ cup milk
1 cup persimmon pulp
1 egg, beaten
1 tablespoon melted butter
1 teaspoon vanilla

METHOD

Sift the dry ingredients.

Mix milk, persimmon and egg, then add melted butter and vanilla.

Combine dry ingredients with the persimmon mixture.

Spread in a shallow buttered pan and bake in a 180°C oven for 30 minutes or until firm and brown.

Cut in squares.

Serve warm with whipped cream.

Pru's praline

INGREDIENTS

2 tablespoons butter
4 tablespoons white or malt vinegar
8 tablespoons sugar

METHOD

Place all ingredients in a saucepan, and slowly cook until the mixture becomes dark golden. Test by dropping a little portion into cold water until it becomes crunchy.

Tip mixture onto a tray lined with baking paper and let it cool until it sets to a brittle consistency.

Put another layer of baking paper on top and hit it with a rolling pin or a bottle until you are no longer angry and the brittle is crushed.

Keep in an airtight jar until ready to use.

Serve on top of fruit, gateaux or other sweet dishes.

Molten mud chocolate pudding in a mug

INGREDIENTS

¼ cup plain flour
2 tablespoons cocoa
½ teaspoon baking powder
3 tablespoons sugar
1 pinch salt
3 tablespoons unsalted butter (melted)
3 tablespoons milk
1 egg
Vanilla
Chocolate bits
1 tablespoon of water

METHOD

In a mug, place wet ingredients into the dry and mix gently.

Add about a dozen chocolate bits in the middle.

Add 1 tablespoon of cold water over the top.

Put in microwave and cook on high for ½ minute.

Serve with raspberries and fresh cream.

Two-minute muffins

INGREDIENTS

1 large handful of sultana bran flakes,
1½ cups milk
Cinnamon and vanilla to taste
1 egg, beaten
½ banana, mashed
1½ cups of self-raising flour
Large handful of fruit medley

METHOD

Place all ingredients into a bowl, folding in the flour last.

Place a quarter of the mixture in a microwave-safe muffin container of approximately ½ cup capacity. Cook in microwave on high for no longer than 2 minutes. Repeat three times to make four muffins in total.

BEER CAKE

TAKE 3 CUPS S.R. FLOUR ADD
3/4 CUP SUGAR: RUB IN 2 TABLSP
BUTTER. ADD 2 CUPS MIXED FRUIT.
POUR IN 1/2 BOT BEER AND
1 BEATEN EGG MIX TO POUR
ING CONSISTENCY PLACE IN
2 or 3 SHALLOW BAKING DISHES
SPRINKLE STREUSEL on TOP —:
1 CUP SUGAR 1 CUP PLAIN FLOUR 1/4 LB
BUTTER MIXED TO CRUMBLE
BAKE FAIRLY HOT OVEN 15-20 MINS

Pru's beer cake

THE CROQUEMBOUCHE MAN

I went straight from my 'doing' behaviour, to extreme obsessive, needy behaviour. Ego rushed back in the shape of the Croquembouche Man.

He was a French photographer, cook, raconteur, con man, playmate, and sex maniac. I did not ask him to the island. He came over with an old friend of mine for a quick visit, but he wanted to stay on. I gave him a definite 'no'. Four days later, I was awaiting the arrival of Nick, who was down for the weekend, and through the door came not only Nick, but also Croquembouche. He had booked himself on the little Cessna run by Emu Airways, and it just happened that Nick was on the same plane. Croquembouche ended up asking how to get to Belinda's. Was it divine intervention or fate that brought him to my door?

I really did not want his intrusion, but I gave in, and immersed myself in the craziest trip of my life.

Croquembouche, as the sweet extravaganza implies, was exotic and fanciful; a multi-layered French pastry in human form. He took over the kitchen, sweets being his forte. He built my mother a huge vegetable garden, me a cocktail bar on the edge of the ocean, fished for bream in the river with a bamboo stick and caught wild geese in his bare hands for 'Prune', as he called my mother, who just adored him. He entertained our guests, my family, and most of all me with physical and mental acrobatics. I had a playmate, a gourmet and a lover all rolled into one. Every sense of myself was brought to the fore. It was '*la grande amour*'.

My mother thought he had come from deep space. Everyone found him fascinating, except Rachel, who was the only one to see the under-story and not be taken in by him. The under-story was that he was crazy. I only experienced a 'fine kind of madness' on Kangaroo Island. But nine months later, on his return to France, I decided to visit him and it was quite a different story.

I was invited to Russia to cook at the embassy in Moscow. Our family had known Charles Robin Ashwin – always known as Robin – since he was a small boy. I got to meet him years later when he married Okche, came to Adelaide and Kangaroo Island, and took the position of Australian Ambassador in Moscow. On one of their trips out, they had this notion I should drop in on my way to France, stay at the embassy, and help the Russian cooks prepare and create a sumptuous grand dinner for about forty invited dignitaries.

I had very little income at this point in my life, hence my disastrous encounter with Aeroflot. The particular model that I picked up in the Middle East looked like something out of the Second World War. I only had half a seatbelt and water dripped on my head from the air conditioner in the bulkhead. For a start, the flight took twice the time with five stops and hours waiting for refuelling. In my boredom and frustration, I decided to drink vodka and consume the only food offered, cold chicken salad and pickles. Big mistake. I was almost strip searched and was only saved by the embassy driver who picked me up and whisked me through customs without my luggage that had been lost as well. What a contrast it was to go from this third-world travel to the inner sanctum of the embassy and the arms of Okche and Robin.

Robin Ashwin, waiting to get bread in Moscow

They were simply wonderful and so was the embassy, with Art Deco ceilings about twenty metres high, beautiful carvings and enormous spaces, grand entertainment areas, and my room, as big as the whole house I live in now.

Straight away I went off to the Russian Ballet and the next day I took a tour of Moscow and the markets. Okche and Robin welcomed me into their lives. They gave me the lowdown on the events that would lead up to the grand dinner, which was to take place two days before I was to leave for Paris. This was the era of food restrictions and literally queues of people lining up for bread. I actually found it very uncomfortable to be led in the back door of the bakery to collect our order while out at the front were dozens of faces pressed to the windows and behind them hundreds more waiting for the shop to open. The supermarkets were no better as they were practically empty of produce. How was I going to invent a menu when there was nothing to cook with? As it turned out, I never found out.

Getting on to the third day, I suddenly felt a weird sensation – a tingling in my arms – and then I felt faint and extremely nauseated. I could not stand up. Hot and cold flushes consumed my body and I put myself to bed, hoping it would pass. But it just got worse and worse. I could not move and I was terrified. The banquet was only one day away. What was I to do? Well, it was obvious that there was no way I could fulfil my obligation in the kitchen. I hardly remember the next day and night, only the vision of Okche coming into my room on the night of the dinner in the most beautiful, creamy silk gown to assure me it was all okay. They had been able to manage without me. It was obvious I had dysentery from the chicken I ate on the Aeroflot. Somehow I managed to get myself well enough to meet the deadline for the flight from Russia to Paris. It was all a blur till I arrived, then Croquembouche was at the airport to greet me.

I was completely depleted of energy and sustenance and gloomy about my health, which was not made any better by the dreadful little hotel

Croquembouche at his castle in France

we stayed in that night and the long trip to Villereversure, a country town. All I remember was a blurred memory of hopeless despair topped only by our arrival in Villereversure and Croquembouche's supposed mansion. The mansion was a demolition site set in the centre of a very pretty little town. All that was livable was a tiny kitchenette, bedroom – all one beige colour – and an outhouse where Mousse slept, which seemed an appropriate culinary name. Mousse was an unidentified human being who seemed to be Croquembouche's lackey. Delusions of grandeur, I would say.

Mousse was not my main concern. My concern was Croquembouche. He was in complete turmoil. He had spoken so often of his grandmother who had brought him up since his father had stabbed him with a pair of scissors and nearly killed him when he was six years old. Croquembouche had especially planned his trip back to France to be with his grandmother and she had not been well. She died before he arrived home. It completely devastated an already unhinged and distraught individual. He was no more the exotic French dynamo I had known on Kangaroo Island, and this was not the beautiful bridge between Australia and France. It was a nightmare that had just begun.

I managed to inflame the situation by questioning the story that he had previously told me. To try and quieten him down, I agreed to take a motorbike ride (a short one, I thought), to see the sights around his village. Instead, we took a wild trip around the mountains and valleys, with me absolutely terrified, clinging on behind. He stopped once in the next hour and a half to show me the castle he said he owned. It was a ruin, a couple of walls and a turret. That evening I woke up in the middle of the night to find him sneaking around the bedroom, swearing in French, claiming someone had stolen his belt! I was not well in my body, and his brain had gone. I was miles away from anywhere and did not even have access to a phone. I was not left alone for a second. I did have plenty of time to think, though. Croquembouche spent all his days working on the renovations while I sat around. If I had not brought my mobile piano, I do not know how I would have spent my time. The only diversion was my suggestion we go out to dine at Paul Bocuse's not far away (on me, of course!). What splendiferous surroundings, but I could not appreciate the true value of the experience since my only diet so far had been rice and bananas.

A day after that, a miracle occurred. Croquembouche had to go out for concrete, usually Mousse's job. I was standing by the telephone wondering whom I could contact when it rang. Something caused me to pick it up and I could not believe there was an American voice on the other end. It was someone I actually knew – a lawyer friend of Croquembouche whom I'd met in Australia and who had visited me on Kangaroo Island. I did not give him a moment to talk. I just explained my position and stressed I had to get away and asked, could he help me? Tony thought of a plan. In three days he would come from Burgundy where he was staying. I would suggest I needed medical attention and would ask if he could drive me to Paris for a couple of days to get treatment. He hung up minutes before Croquembouche returned, then rang again pretending it was his first call. Those three days seemed an eternity. Eventually, Tony arrived and Croquembouche put on a special banquet to impress him. My contribution was an enormous jar of caviar I had brought from Russia.

Not soon enough it was time to leave with the promise I would be back. Once I got in the car I downloaded the entire trauma and the awful truth about Croquembouche, whom Tony had known for years. As Villereversure vanished from sight, I began to relax. Luckily, Tony owned a castle in Burgundy that he shared with a couple of gay friends and we could stay the night there before leaving for Paris. It was an extraordinary culture shock arriving at a huge, real, turreted castle with everything intact. We had a very sumptuous meal. The four of us were actually analysing the Croquembouche phenomenon when the phone rang. It was him! He had suspected we were there and decided he would join us. This time Tony was very concerned and insisted we leave straight away. It was only when we got back in the car that he told me of a past incident when a girlfriend of Croquembouche had moved out and he had chased her all the way to Paris with a gun.

Tony had an apartment just next to the Eiffel Tower in one of those beautiful Parisian blocks with the little balconies. I experienced a real sense of Paris. What a relief! At least I felt safe there. He recommended I did not leave the apartment while he was at work, and in the evenings he took me to wonderful places to eat. I paid with gratitude. On the morning of my departure to Australia, I rang Croquembouche and all I said was, 'I am sorry, this was not a beautiful bridge to your country. I do not ever want to see or hear from you again. I am leaving today.' I hung up in his ear.

I cannot tell you how many times he rang me in Australia and how many years after that he pleaded with my mother to make me speak to him. I never did. I usually accept apologies but I am especially weak when it comes to lustful encounters.

I then made an attempt to return to the 'being' life on Kangaroo Island.

CULINARY CAPERS ACROSS AMERICA

Rachel, in the meantime, was safely six months into her trip away. She was now nineteen. I was no longer her boss and I did not know how to reinvent myself as her mother and as her friend. She had come up with a plan to deliver cars across America. It started out as a simple and inexpensive idea to see the country, so the idea to join my daughter partway through her year of exploration seemed a great way to reconnect.

We travelled on Route 66. It was a hot summer. We were on a journey that not only took us across America from east to west, but north to south as well. Rachel had taken on the job of delivering cars well before I arrived to meet up with her. She had already been from New York to Los Angeles and was on her way to pick me up in San Francisco, with plans of delivering a new car to Tallahassee. The car company deal required a large bond up front on departure. The bond was refundable if the car was okay at the destination. We paid for the petrol and had to stick to a pre-planned route.

Rachel was in charge of our adventure. I felt it was certainly her turn for my attention. Her research was by means of her $5-per-day guidebook. It was such a treat to meet with her on foreign ground. A bit of spoiling went on when we got to San Francisco and I made sure we had a great hotel and plenty of lovely food. We gorged ourselves on strawberries the size of apples and seafood on the pier, and we visited an extraordinary selection of eateries chosen by Rachel. We walked all the way to every one of them. Once we had our bearings, we moved to Haight Ashbury, the old hippy quarter of the 1970s, into a very famous hotel called the Red Victorian and joined the Festival of Music and Food that takes place there every year. It was the most amazing street party. We thought it was very funny that we were presumed lesbians, not mother and daughter. We played along until it was time to meet up with Kashka, an old friend of mine from my last trip to America.

Kashka came from a large African-American family in Oakland.

I had stayed with his girlfriend Lily White when I was last visiting Los Angeles. Kashka wanted to give Rachel and me a treat before we started our driving trip. He was an actor and hairdresser and was best friends with Danny Glover. His favourite pastimes were salsa dancing, reading spiritual books and visiting hot and cold springs up in the mountains and we did all of these things with him. It was an extraordinary experience for both of us. We ended up visiting his family and sticking to the plastic furniture covers when it was 40 degrees. We cooked a feast for them as a thank you and ended up staying the night, with Rachel and me floating around together on their huge waterbed.

It was now time to leave San Francisco and pick up our car, which was not very new, I might add, and deliver it to Tallahassee. Only one day later, just out of Palm Springs, I lay staring up at the star-studded ceiling of the Starlight Motel waiting for Rachel to come back and tell me if she was able to get a part for the car. This was the first of many problems and stops we encountered along the way. There were truck stops, roadhouses, car repairs and cheap hotels to navigate. We became 'roadie gals'. Rachel started talking like a Texan and confused everyone.

The further we travelled the harder it got. Turning back was not an option and the car company informed us that we could not leave the car behind. Each time we had another hold-up, we invented another new verse of 'On the Road Again'. To make matters worse, I left my passport in a forest cabin in Flagstaff and only realised a day and a half later. We were on a tight schedule but we nonetheless had to backtrack (passing the Grand Canyon twice with no time to stop), retrieve it and make it to Phoenix. By this time we were down to staying in backpackers' hostels.

One memorable night in New Mexico in a heat wave, Rachel took her bed clothes out on the roof, put toilet paper in her ears and secured a chair so she could sleep without falling off the roof, while I stayed inside in a bed where the pillows smelt of a thousand smelly heads. We gave ourselves a treat in Sedona, the spiritual centre of Arizona and the

Me at the hostel in New Mexico where Rachel slept on the roof

home of crystals, mystics and powwows. We did it all. We stayed in a beautiful motel looking down into a canyon and this is where Rachel invented 'bed aerobics'. After being in a car for all those hours every day we became quite unfit, so Rachel created an exercise that entailed lying flat on our backs in bed and attempting to lift our whole bodies off at the same time while clapping our hands beneath us. All it did was awaken the people sleeping below, who bashed on the ceiling with a broom to shut us up.

Spiritual sisters was the best role we had played so far. Back on the road again, however, this trip had become a nightmare in travelling, only relieved by the truly wonderful, eccentric, hospitable and respectable folk we met along the way. Nothing was too much trouble. If we got lost, they took us to the right turn-off. They laughed with us and at us, and befriended us. On the other hand, our food experiences were a disaster. We ate fast foods I had never seen before, accompanied by all styles of Deb mashed potatoes, shiny brown gravy and fat-infused oddities on overloaded plates that could have fed six people. It was at this point that we came to honour the wonders of popcorn.

We travelled from then on in a wake of popcorn, bound for El Paso on the Mexican border. We had a faulty ignition now and one day, when the temperature was 104, we were freewheeling down hill and dale when suddenly the air conditioner gave up and the radiator ran dry. Our car died at the bottom of the hill and we had no way to continue. There were the two of us, miles from nowhere, red hills as far as the eye could see and wild winds tossing up the spinifex grasses. In the distance we could make out something that looked like a movie set in an old western – an empty shop attached to an old shed. Our car rolled to a halt a few hundred metres from the verandah. There was not a sign of life until Rachel went around the back where four Vietnam veterans were playing cards. They were not very friendly and we were very uncomfortable. They did give us water, enough for the radiator and some to put over our heads as we limped into El Paso. This had to be the end of the car, the road and the end of nowhere!

Last stop before breakdown and on to El Paso

What a godforsaken place. A town set beside a huge grey mountain with grey drab buildings stretching to the border of Mexico. The car company wanted to fix the car but it couldn't be done and so they gave us no alternative but a bus ride out of there. We stayed one night in a crummy hotel where Rachel looked in her $5-per-day book for a Mexican treat. She decided on the 'Tap'. We ordered a taxi and a very pleasant Lebanese chap suggested that we not go to the Tap in downtown El Paso. But Rachel had made up her mind. Oh dear! On entering, we were seated in a restaurant packed full of men. We were the only two women in the place and there seemed to be a thousand dark eyes staring at us.

Almost instantly a table of three men (not Mexican) moved in on us. They were not unpleasant but kept insisting that we go across the Mexican border with them to visit. We would have never got back – we were now the whores of El Paso! We were literally chased out of the doors and into the back seat of a cab – the same nice Lebanese guy had waited outside. From that moment on we followed his guide, just waiting until we were able to leave on the bus. He was a miracle in a moment of Mexican madness.

We got a bus to Phoenix and then we decided that air travel might suit us better. Where to now, Rachel? Together we decided to fly to Memphis and Nashville and follow the trail of Elvis Presley, Jimmy Hendrix and B.B. King down in Beale Street. Then we hired a car and went south through Oprah Winfrey country and the Grand Ole Opry for music festivals. Memphis and Nashville were music to our ears. We just loved the history. In that part of the world, music came nearly on par with food and since we had not been having much luck in that direction, we soaked up all that we could in street music and cocktail bars. Wine was very expensive in those days – cocktails were the 'in' thing – so we managed to sometimes take one drink from place to place to avoid extreme prices. We were bold and brash. In hindsight I should have pulled back and paid attention to our safety as things went from normal to bizarre and then to really scary on our trip down south.

We had done limited research and little planning to take us through the rest of our journey. To be fair though, the change of plans at El Paso was not our fault and I feel we had lost our sense of direction. Eventually we decided to follow up a contact we had from Kashka in Baton Rouge. It should have been a warning to go back when we got lost on the bridge into town, in the dark. Around and around we went, missing all the turn-offs, back again to the pay station, and we were running out of cash. 'How do we get off this bridge?' The lady at the toll station was not helpful. It was late, dark and frustrating. It was too late to find our contact and we needed somewhere to stay for the night. A neon sign directed us to Ramada Inn. It looked run-down, outdated and empty and we were worn out, tired and hungry. Rachel consulted her guidebook. 'Hey Ma, did you know this was the town they filmed *Sex, Lies and Videotapes* in? The pub is just around the corner. Let's go and have a quick look'.

We took off down the street and walked into the saloon bar where there was a party going on. It was fun and relaxing and we mingled and met some really great people. We enjoyed a counter meal and suddenly it was 1.00 am. Back at the Ramada, things were pretty quiet. We put our noses into the bar, as one last drink was just what we needed. Somehow we got separated and just after that a very scrappy, most unattractive guy approached me. 'Would I like a massage?' I declined and immediately found Rachel and told her I would quietly slip away to my room. As she was not ready to come to bed, I gave her a key and told her I would leave the chain off.

Relief at last, I was safe in bed and nearly asleep when I heard the key in the lock. I thought it was Rachel, but seconds later I felt strong hands on my shoulders and a voice, which said, 'Don't give me no shit, woman, or there will be trouble.' Fear welled up inside of me. It was that man. How had he got in? What next? What next was obvious, but what was I to do? Run, call out, resist or give in? As Rachel was nowhere to be seen, I gave in to the last option of least resistance, so I could get him out of the room as quick as possible and before Rachel returned. It was all over in a matter of seconds. When I ran away to the bathroom I noticed a big set of keys on the side table. The hotel owners must have employed him.

Moments after that, I heard Rachel at the door and just behind her another employee. Rachel had no idea what was going on but I managed to coax him out of the door quickly. I put on the chain and tried to explain to Rachel what had happened. This was suddenly interrupted by the sound of the door being opened again and they were back, to be faced by the security chain and my face peering through the crack. Whatever I said must have had some effect because they did not break down the door. They left.

Later we discovered Baton Rouge is one of the most dangerous places in North America, worse than New Orleans, with about one murder reported each week. We were lucky to escape with our lives. White women were not respected and we had stayed at a third-class motel in downtown Baton Rouge where HIV was on the increase. One thing we learned on this trip was that downtown anywhere was a recipe for trouble.

There was a shocking epitaph to the Baton Rouge experience. Once the highs and excitement of travelling and reconnecting with my daughter were over, I had to focus on the 'rape' issue. I needed to check with my gynaecologist to make sure all was okay. Tests revealed that I had a mild STD. I felt relief, reflecting back to the down-and-out status and roughness of the man involved in that awful nightmare. I knew it could have been far worse.

Weeks went by, then I started to get weird symptoms such as sore gums, lumps and, what was worse, a serious rash down my back. As I had been down the gynaecological road before, I sought alternative treatments. Eventually a dermatologist cut part of the rash and sent it off to the lab. There were no positive results. I became very sick. Help came in the form of my friend Peter, a doctor who lived in the church next door. He ran more tests, and the results came back almost immediately. I had advanced syphilis! What was a white Australian upper-crust socialite doing with a disease of this nature? I spent over three weeks at the clinic, an adventure in itself. I had penicillin and a complex cocktail of drugs till I was clean.

Mismanaged treatment was only one aspect of what came out of all of this. It had a very personal effect on both Rachel and me. She was only nineteen. It really revealed to me how easily trouble can arrive in unknown places and that I should have been more mindful as a mother. My excuse is I really wanted, just once, to let Rachel take charge. At Jolley's I was her boss and her mother and I wanted this time for it to be different.

Rachel 'in charge' did come later, in the nicest and most positive way possible. She introduced me to both Buddhism and Bikram yoga. She literally forced me to attend yoga during an accident-prone era on Kangaroo Island. She walked me there three times a week. She made me stay in the room at forty-two degrees. It nearly killed me. But a miracle occurred. It healed all the past accidents, especially my ankles, which were very weak. Rachel was my physical and mental guru. She became a teacher of Power Flow yoga – a star in both teaching and meditation.

Yoga became an intrinsic part of my life from that time on, especially important to my physical wellbeing. It has left an imprint on my body memory. Once you know the practice, it is forever with you and you can slot right back into it at any time. From Bikram, I transferred to other yoga disciplines until I found my centre in Yin yoga, which is similar in postures but different in its slow and sustained techniques that strengthen without the physical extremes of heat and dynamics. Anyone is capable of this practice. It can be done at home or on your own, backed up with your favourite music. Yoga used to be a 'woo woo' word but now it is a 'wow wow' word.

The other real connection of significance was Buddhism. When

Rachel moved to Melbourne to follow her culinary career, she had her own mentor, teacher and mother substitute in Theresa. She really found her heart and connection there. I joined her for the visits of the Dalai Lama. I loved these visits. We had a special link at last. Because of Theresa and her Buddhist studies Rachel was asked to cook for the Dalai Lama at the four-day public meetings in Melbourne. You will never guess what he requested: spaghetti bolognese.

RACHEL'S STORY

Mum asked me if I would define my concept of 'sourcing the sauce' and my thinking about how I connect it to my relationship with Buddhism.

With a childhood based in a family of creative freaks, years of running restaurants and time spent playing as a drummer in a rock band, the Buddhist essence and creative thinking have never been far from my life.

My journey of challenges (which each and every one of us has) is really defined by the Buddhist studies that I have explored for the last twenty-five years. My passion in this pursuit came about when I grew disappointed with certain outcomes in my life. I was trying to control and manage life in a seemingly chaotic world of fate vs time. The result was everything I was doing was meaningless.

I learned that Buddhist practices were all about cutting back delusions or false thinking, while simultaneously developing warmness for others. Developing compassion for others actually improves one's ability to develop wisdom. Such thinking certainly piqued my interest. In fact, according to Buddhist thought, the pure wisdom gained at enlightenment is not possible without the perfection of generosity and compassion. Think about that! Compassion is also about revealing our true nature, which, according to Buddhist thought, is in and of itself pure, wise and totally perfect. I am still struggling with this notion. Self-perception, for me, is hard to work on. I am aware that most people are generally hard on himself or herself, and I am still a part of this group.

In theory, this all sounds great. But on reflection of the challenges and the rocky path of life travelled by Mum and others and shared in this book, it is clear to me that everyone is really looking for meaning. In general we are all trying to find ways to dodge hardships and pain in any form. For me it is the same.

In Buddhism there are three types of pain: physical, mental and all-pervasive, which is the pain of searching for meaning with an undertone of never being satisfied – craving, if you like.

The big questions I always ask myself remain: why do things fall apart? Why is half the population medicated? Why has the vision I had of life turned out to be not what I expected? Why am I here? Why am I successful and still not happy?

My personal exploration of answers to these questions raised me from the grind of daily life to new views and perspectives. After all, my experience of life is mostly about my mental perception.

Today, I believe that if I pick something that I want to make work and practise it with effort and diligence, it will be tough but I will succeed. I am often asked how I've endured some of the very difficult times that have been presented to me. I always give credit to Buddhist practice. It's like medicine. Once applied it will take effect. That's what being human is. A wonderful teacher whom I went on a mission to find, in my twenties, has defined me. She drummed into me to not just read about the meditation but to apply it! I can hear her now getting frustrated with me when I forgot to embody the practice. Taking action eventually improves one's mind and one's mind will eventually improve the actions.

Buddhism is the complete meal for me. There is a practice for every disposition. Only catch is ... you must do the work!

RACHEL – THE OTHER SIDE

There was still something left in revelations; I should have twigged.

Rachel was a well-established heavy rock drummer at the age of nineteen and she was in two bands, the Coneheads and Muff. So I should not have been surprised when she wrote to me to say that she was gay.

I had already established a special place in Adelaide's gay community. I loved that environment. It felt like a comfortable place to be after the end of my marriage. I felt sensual, not sexually attacked. I went to all their parties. I could dress up outrageously and dance the night away, with someone always stealing my stilettos, as my feet are enormous.

When I received Rachel's letter to say she was gay, it was a different story. This was my own daughter. The moment I read it, I decided it was very personal. This was my fault. I felt guilt for leaving my marriage and all my subsequent parenting issues. Even worse was the fact that homosexuality was a taboo subject for our wider family, as were Jews, blacks and Catholics! I made very sure the family did not find out for years.

At the same time, I tried my best to integrate with Rachel's community. When asked, I went to gigs; I had dinners with her and her girlfriends. But anxiety ruled supreme. It was lucky that I was on Kangaroo Island and Rachel was living in Adelaide and Melbourne during this period. A lot later, when Rachel's partner, whom I loved, became enmeshed in part of the Kangaroo Island business, the addition of another entity to the family pot caused dissension, but it was really not about sexual orientation.

Thank goodness, I have overcome those initial issues and today I accept what is and what is meant to be. It has not changed one aspect of Rachel, her true nature, or how much I love her.

SO, WHAT ABOUT NICK?

Nick recalls his 'summer of innocence' story in his own words. It is the story of childhood memories, back in the 1980s, that he wants to tell.

NICK'S STORY

At the age of fourteen the long summers on Kangaroo Island were about fun, freedom, friends and endless sunburn. During the school holidays we slipped into a perpetual hedonistic existence that was worlds away from the strict school routines, homework and bedtime curfew of 8 pm.

Each day on my blissful island I was up at sunrise, eager to spend every waking moment on the beach, fishing or exploring the sand hills. I was not seen by my parents until I became hungry or it got dark at the end of the day.

One summer my older cousins from Sydney, Seb and James, came to visit with their posse of rambunctious mates who would smoke endless packets of Benson and Hedges and pot. They continually oiled their buffed bodies between swims on the beach.

Being fourteen, and part of the younger group, I remember looking up to the older boys and thinking how cool they were. Their night-time games of spin the bottle and schwartz (a drinking game) combined with moon-lit boating trips and secret rendezvous with their girlfriends was enticing and exciting.

It was early on in the holidays of 1985 when we discovered an old thatched house in the sand hills behind Snellings Beach. It sat on a bend in Middle River and off to one side was a collection of small rooms that were made from corrugated iron and heavily painted in yellow ochre. Each room had big heavy bolted doors, very little light and was lined with old wire beds and hammocks. When you opened the door for the first time the salty air smelt dank and stale. I remember entering with cautious steps, thinking it felt like a prison cell.

One of the main games introduced to us this summer was initiated by my cousin Seb, who was about twenty-one at the time. It involved hypnotising a group of us and then making us do silly things in front of the group.

It all seemed like harmless fun.

Not shy of attention, I thought it would be fun to pretend I was hypnotised and act out the commands that were put upon me. I remember pretending to go into a trance to then perform the acts he called out, like, 'Have a fight with a pole. When you wake up, you'll jump up and down ten times every ten minutes.' To shrieks of laughter I became the star of the show that summer.

From here things suddenly got very dark. In one session with me, Seb created a special word that he could later use at any time to put me into an instant hypnotic state again. This new addition to Seb's show would take the performance to a whole new level, enabling Seb to control me and the performance at a whim, any time of the day and in front of any unsuspecting crowd.

One afternoon I came up from the beach by myself to relax in one of the hammocks until Seb quietly entered the room. Without a warning he said the trigger word. With no audience I was confused. It was just Seb and me. I did not want go under his spell but it would be worse for me to reveal I was making the whole thing up. So on cue I started the act and pretended I was under hypnosis.

He came over close to me, and said I would remember nothing, I felt his breath close to my mouth, I remember the strong smell of Blue Stratos aftershave and then I felt his bristly mouth kiss me.

The moment was brief. However, I felt a wash of confusion flood my brain, not being able to process what happened. When he took me out of the supposed hypnotic state, I found myself scrambling to get back into character and pretend that nothing had happened. This was a harder act to perform than the crazy acts I was asked to play out for the crowds.

I saw on Seb's face that he knew he had got away with it. And for the rest of the summer holidays I pushed it out of my mind and tried to keep away from Seb.

With only a few days before the summer holidays were over, I thought I was home and hosed, until one afternoon I went up to our Cliff House after a swim on the beach. It was about 3 pm and no one was in the house so I went to our sunken lounge to chill out. Seb appeared out of nowhere. He must have been watching, and followed me up from the beach. Without any conversation he said the trigger word to me again. This time I did not go under straight away. I was confused. I wanted to let him know it was all a joke but as I only had seconds to decide, I pretended to fall under his spell again because I felt ambushed and, for some reason, embarrassed. When my eyes were closed Seb again commanded that I would not remember anything, before I felt him undoing the front of my shorts and heard him undo his zipper. I was scared frozen.

He proceeded to sexually abuse me.

I had been completely violated. After what would have been a five-minute span, he 'woke' me up, spoke to me as if nothing had happened and went on his merry way.

The holidays ended and I went back to school in Adelaide trying to put the whole experience behind me.

Life was okay for the next few months until I had to return to Kangaroo Island again. I was back at the Cliff House and it made me think about what had happened that summer. Like a switch being flicked, I suddenly felt a barrage of emotions and negative thoughts that I had no capacity to deal with.

I thought I had turned gay, or I was gay. This thought horrified me because the act made me feel ashamed and dirty. I questioned why I let Seb do it. Did that mean I had liked it? I started to fall into a deep depression. It was like a virus that had infected my brain. Each day got worse. For the first time in my life, I looked forward to bedtime so

I could give my mind a rest from the worry and negative thoughts of the day. The moment I woke up each morning I was back in my real-life nightmare. It never left my thoughts.

Slowly the world lost its colour. The trees and birds meant nothing to me. I felt no emotion. I had no interest in food, friends or life. I felt numb. What was the point? I just wanted to escape my mind, which meant sleep or die.

Out of desperation, I remember calling Mum in Adelaide, as she was not on the island at the time. She immediately told me to come back to Adelaide.

After a couple of sessions with a therapist, I saw a crack of light in the distance, but despite seeing that possibility of hope, I had no idea how to make the light grow. Around this time Mum contacted her clairvoyant friend Louie Mascara. Although Mum might have wanted my future predicted in an easy nutshell, for me it was Louie's guidance about understanding the process of 'thought' that helped me map out a path to recovery.

Mum may not have known it at the time but I believe that her intuition about tapping into the source and believing in me ultimately saved my life.

By connecting me with Louie I was able to find the source of the infection in my brain, and by using repetitive positive thoughts and processes I built a healthy mindset from the inside out.

This was not a fast process, but as the months went past my hope for happiness started to grow. I noticed that I could go half a day without negative thoughts about the abuse, then a week, and then months. After a few years, I was able to let negative memories come and go without effect. I had the power. I was in control of my own mind. It was an exhilarating feeling.

From here came strength. I found I was able to talk to other people about my experience; I was even able to contact Seb as an adult and confront him about what he had done to me.

I wanted to share this story in Mum's book because I think it's hugely important to initiate open discussions about child abuse if we are to have any chance of shifting the power away from the abuser and bringing it back to the victim. I am now an artist, entrepreneur, husband, father of three beautiful boys, and I am not and never have been defined by my abuse. But I have lived it and recovered from it because I was believed, protected and supported in getting help by those around me. I want people to know that this is the first and best thing you can do for someone who discloses sexual, physical or emotional abuse. And I want people to know that you can have a wonderful, rich life after going through abuse.

Once Nick realised it was not going to work for him at Jolley's with the new management, and that we had to sell Palmer Place to pay out Ian for the Cliff House, he moved far, far away. I took it personally when he moved to Far North Queensland.

He was already an established artist and he was also under the strict guidance of his famous artist uncle, Robert 'Alf' Hannaford. He had also worked from kiosk to front of house at Jolley's and had all the associated skills in hospitality, but he did not have a wife. That was about to change. He met a young girl from the Isle of Man, Amelia, who was in Australia on holidays. She followed him north to the Whyanbeel Valley on the edge of the Daintree where they started a business selling cappuccinos and black bamboo artifacts, which they made themselves, at the Sunday markets in Port Douglas.

Amelia's parents are aristocratic and eccentric and very English, and were therefore very unsure of the suitability of a feral, colonial boy from Aussie-land being a good match for their daughter. In fact, Amelia's mother was so worried she went to her resident clairvoyant and expressed her fear of Amelia marrying Nick. Her reply was, 'She already has married him!'

On my brief visit to Far North Queensland, not more than six months after they had been together, Nick and Amelia asked me if I would help them get married. They needed me since Amelia was only on a tourist visa. Of course I agreed. The marriage took place in a matter of days. A coal-fired train took the three of us down to Port Douglas. Crisp white turned to black soot. We lost the celebrant. There was one bridesmaid with a video camera strapped to her head and two drunken fishermen as witnesses. After the wedding we had a dinner for four at a smart Port Douglas restaurant.

Back on the Isle of Man, Amelia's parents (Sir Quentin and April Agnew Somerville) went into shock when they found out. They announced there would be a formal wedding, a grand production for hundreds. It was the most bizarre wedding I have ever been to. Amelia wore navy blue velvet. Nick wore a green velveteen smoking jacket. The bridesmaids, six of them, all made and designed their own dresses, fashioned in gold lame. I had never seen so much aristocracy in one gathering.

Back in Far North Queensland, Amelia's dislike for me was palpable. Subsequent visits were uncomfortable and what did not help the situation was that there was nowhere for me to sleep other than on top of the shed in the garden that housed Piggie. Piggie was a 'miniature pig' that grew to weigh 400 kg, so it could not live with Nick and Amelia in their house. Here was I on a platform of fly wire and tin on a tiny bit of foam for a mattress. I named my residence 'The Last Resort', which was the first of many throughout my life.

It really did become the best resort after Nick and Amelia had Darcy, their son. Darcy is a book in himself. I hope one day Nick will write about Darcy. He has survived the most severe case of cerebral palsy, which could have been avoided had it not been for their hippy doctor pushing for a natural birth in the middle of nowhere. Darcy cannot speak, eat, or move without a wheelchair and even that is difficult as he is so heavy. Amelia has an intensive care unit set up in her house

Nick and Piggie

where he lives. He has multiple and severe problems that put Amelia and her partner on alert 24/7. Sadly, Darcy marked the end of Nick and Amelia's marriage.

At the same time, Nick and Amelia had created the most amazing business, Hannaford's Special Events, with creative, inventive, magical experiences: dinners in the rainforest, on beaches, floating down rivers or even set up on a sandy cay in the middle of the ocean.

One day, the council rang Nick and said they had some VIP guests they wanted to bring for a meal in the rainforest. At that time, Nick had no kitchen and was nervous about bringing council people out for a meal. He made an excuse that he had family commitments. The council would not give up since Hannaford's Special Events was so well respected. After much toing and froing, the council revealed the guests' names to twist Nick's arm – Mick and Bianca Jagger! That got things moving. Nick decided to set up a table and mobile kitchen away from the house and next to the river with candelabras swinging from the trees, complete with a jungle man swinging through the branches. There were just six of them. It was a feast to behold. Mick and Bianca were insistent that Nick get some mangosteens from the forest for them to take home. In his haste, he slipped down the hill and broke his leg and landed at the feet of Bianca. What a special place to end up!

I loved being up there with Darcy around those times. When Amelia revealed she was having an affair, Nick moved away. He opened an arm of their events business in Sydney. I am pleased that any sadness and suffering that Nick may have encountered has been counterbalanced now that Nick has a wife, Lisa, and two more beautiful children.

Magician Man

Artisan Creative Man
Try and catch him if you can
Many hats, he's in disguise
Chameleon before your eyes!

Magician Man, weave a spell
3D vision, done so well
Of all the boys I've put to test
You're the one I love the best!

BACK TO THE SOURCE

Why has Kangaroo Island played such an important role in my life? It will always represent freedom to me. Maybe part of the appeal is escapism. It certainly was when I was young; escape from school, social pressures, responsibilities and the rules and regulations of Robe Terrace. Now I realise it offers much more than that. It offers space, natural beauty, solitude, and a deep connection to the power of the universe. Through this physicality comes a connection to my source, creating for me a kind of magic. It has taught me how to live without speaking a word, to accept myself, confront deceptions and the truth, and express my creativity. The most important thoughts and moments of true clarity have emerged for me there. I brought my loves to experience the extraordinary energy of this place and to see whether our relationships could survive. Those relationships were always challenging and dynamic. I lost some, found some, demanded far too much from myself and others, but still came back for more.

I first tried to understand what the island really represented for me by writing poems and songs. They came from a source that seemed beyond my conscious mind. I would write words I had no idea the meanings of till I looked them up in the dictionary. The source of my 'being' seemed fascinating and cosy and safe away from public scrutiny, when being in the world physically seemed overwhelming and terrifying.

When I eventually returned to Kangaroo Island for the third long-term stay, I realised something else much more revealing: I had a feeling that my children did not really respect, like or even love me. The one thing I had promised myself in my early teens was that I would get married, have children and be happy forever after, and that I would be the mother my own mother could not be – loving, connected and fun.

In the early years of my children's growing up, I was able to play out my own childhood fantasies with them, but unfortunately when they reached their teens and I was a single mother, things changed. I still wanted to be a playmate in their adventures and my thinking still was, 'I am a wonderful, fun, free-spirited mother. I never hit them or even discipline them very much.' Why would I want them to suffer as we all did as sisters?

However, in hindsight, they were not old enough or strong enough to stand up to my silly behaviour.

HANNAFORDS OF KANGAROO ISLAND

I started Hannafords of Kangaroo Island when the Cliff House, Osprey and the Settlers' Cottage were finished. They were all now rented under this new umbrella. In addition to the accommodation, I created wonderful location dining.

The Fig Tree

The Fig Tree was over 170 years old. I had crawled inside its leafy arms when I was a child. It had expanded and rerooted way back off the road and with a little pruning it turned into the most incredible leafy grotto comprising three rooms of fantasy, fairyland, and *Magic Faraway Tree* experiences. With the help of a one-eyed woodsman with a chainsaw, we crafted a stairway over the trunk leading from one room to the

Mum and me, first opening of the Fig Tree in the 70s

The Shearing Shed

next. With the longest extension cord ever invented, we plugged into the homestead, creating fairy light magic at night.

The Fig Tree was truly a summer haven. What to do in winter? Well, there just happened to be an old shearing shed, out of action since the 1930s, filled up to the roof with sheep shit with no walls but beautiful redgum posts, carrying the marks of counting the sheep. I built a wood fire kiln, new walls of brush and tin, and I traded accommodation and meals for decoration – church pews, old artifacts and even a boat. This beautiful shed became the centre for amazing feasts not dissimilar to those featured in the film *Babette's Feast*.

Nothing was too much trouble in those days. I was experimenting, with no real aim at any particular market. We made wonderful friends. There was a lot of trial and error and we often forgot vital bits of equipment, matches, paper, bottle openers, only to slip away and make trips back to the kitchen in the main house.

Mrs Kitchenhands

Wild pig in kiln experience

Imagine six feet of pig in a kiln set at 400°C stoked all day by my mother with me as a helper.

At 10 am, I opened the door to close the flue section and there was a blast of heat so great it burnt off my eyelashes and grilled the front of my hair to a crisp! Next the pig was too big and heavy for my mum and me to lift up to the opening, which was at chest level. No one was around. What to do? My mother rushed off to get the saw from the shed and single-handedly sawed the beast in half, making it possible to lift each half and stuff them in together. Everything from there on was in the lap of the gods. There was no way to check the cooking process. No way to control the temperature. We could only hope.

Later there followed excitement and relief – not only was the pig cooked to perfection, but it was covered with crisp pork crackling. My hair and red eyeballs did not get a mention!

Nick's Knob

The next extreme location was Nick's Knob, designated during a lunch with my son Nick. I had a very special friend called Pam Cleland who taught me the only subject I passed at school: art. We have kept up the most incredible connection till this day – socially, creatively and philosophically. She's the epitome of things I admire creatively and she was also a smart lawyer. It was on one of her trips to Kangaroo Island that Nick and I invented a lunch for her which none of us would ever forget.

There was a special spot along the coast that had incredible energy, away from the main business, along an old rocky sheep track, high above the ocean. We decided to have a progressive lunch and set up three spots along the way to our lunch destination. I went ahead with the food while Nick chauffeured Pam in the antique Land Cruiser 'cocktail truck' to where I was waiting, We sat together and Nick looked like a character from *Deliverance*. I had on an old Russian army

Mink coats Stellato's Boppa's chops at Nicks Knob.

Fighting the Fox Fur.

coat from the disposals shop and Pam had on a white mink coat and the highest stilettos.

Our final destination was Nick's choice. It was on top of a five-by-five-metre rocky outcrop, high above the sea. There were sheer rocks on three sides and an unbelievable view of coastline as far as the eye could see.

It was simple fare: middle loin chops, cooked in an invention of my father's – a hinged wire grill with screwed-up newspaper as the only fuel in a fire chamber that was an old cast-iron lavatory system, with holes letting in the air. With the chops we served a simple fresh salad and hot English mustard. The three of us sat at a little table teetering on the edge of what could be a disaster. Then Pamela said, 'Lucky I have on my stilettos, so I can spike myself into the ground in case I sneeze and blow myself off the cliff!'

We had such a day. We left Nick back at the homestead and I drove the car onto the beach and fell into the sea that looked just like the champagne we had been drinking. The last memory I have is of Pam and me on two steamer chairs – me still in my army coat and Pam (God knows where it came from) clad in a pink chenille dressing gown.

The Taverna

The beach tavern came about after my father died and we changed the old boatshed he rented off the Harbours Board into a new meal spot. We now had a mountaintop, a fig tree and a shearing shed – why not a tavern on the beach to remind me of Italy and Greece? It was a cheaper alternative than a trip away.

MATES RETURN

With Hannafords of Kangaroo Island, the Inner and Outer Mates came back with a vengeance. This time it was the WWOOFers (Workers Wanted On Organic Farms, or World Wide Opportunities on Organic Farms). They came from foreign countries, travellers looking for board and keep in exchange for work. One or two Inner Mates lived in the flat attached to my mother's homestead while the Outer Mates lived just down the road and became part of our family.

Everyone had a nickname. First a young farmer that my mother adored and named Goddo because every time she broke down, backed into someone, or equipment failed, he was always just around the corner. He in turn named my mother Turbo, and me Whirly Bird, a very apt combination of my 'bird' status and tendency to hover around like an out-of-control helicopter.

There was Girlie, Flatty, Skippy, Dan the Man, Mrs P, King of Tides and Prince of Dolphins to name a few and then the renaming of Middle River to Middle Kingdom. I wrote poems about them. One comes to mind . . .

Food truck for beach events

There was Dan the Man and Mrs P,
Up the road and near to me,
All a force to keep on course.
Greenies, rednecks, fisher-kings,
All became part of our favourite things.
Backpackers, Woofs now part of the team,
All in the mix, rich part of the cream.
Topped off with bubbles (oceans of fun),
Whirly Bird flying, Turbo on the run.
The sauce, the source,
The Yin and Yang,
Hannafords of Kangaroo Island went off with a bang!!

Age: forty-five

We had our team, and I could cook food from any culture and play it out in Middle River, one of the most spectacular locations on earth. We had so much fun in those first years developing the product. Poetry, parties and playtime all became very significant.

Inner and Outer Mates staff on Kangaroo Island

Map of Middle River

I had collected the most amazing collection of dress-ups over the years. There were handmade kimonos, ball gowns encrusted with jewels, wigs, hats and an extensive selection of instruments – an organ, electric piano accordion, African drums and other percussion. These items all helped to create the atmosphere for the feasts we created in the shearing shed.

As one would have detected in the Robe Terrace era, I always seemed to have a cringing fear when it came to the rich and famous, our family being part of that world. I did not respect my heritage and was glad to get lost in the Hannaford lineage when I married. Suddenly, I came to respect the rich and famous in an entirely different way. Kangaroo Island was a perfect setting for those people to spend their summer holidays. I suppose it was to do with the fact that everything now was on my terms, up to a point. I was able to introduce them to the magic of Kangaroo Island, the beautiful settings and locations on offer. It was our 'Little Kingdom' and quietly I imagined I was the ruler, beyond my mother's 'Lady' status.

Our new guests became addicted to Kangaroo Island and their regular Christmas bookings. Every New Year's Eve, they were nearly queueing, on the phone after midnight to book for the following Christmas. Just like with Jolley's, the word spread and the cameras rolled. There were glossy magazine covers, print publicity and television specials, and even a connection to the really true cooking doyennes of the day, Maggie Beer and Stephanie Alexander.

Suddenly all this became a little scary. Was I about to let my ego out again to run havoc? Well, my Buddhist teachings said no! I decided to follow what my true nature was intuitively saying: 'Get with the environment, the locals' needs, the real source inside the crust of Kangaroo Island.'

I did research and talked at council meetings about wanting to start youth programs and at the same time I created a Middle River landcare group, joined Trees for Life, Greening Australia, Save the Glossy Blacks, Coastal Watch and started Coastal Connections, for low-key, eco-friendly accommodation around the coast of Kangaroo Island. I started retreats. Carers' respite weekends became part of the new Di Tong Ling Buddha Centre almost next door. There were yoga classes and cooking classes, and this was when the phrase 'Back to the Source' was first implanted in my brain.

Tree planting became more extensive but funding was scant, so many hours were spent on the bare slopes of Middle River, planting thousands of seed stock. Enter Wayne Brown. He was with the department of agriculture, and saw me struggling to achieve projects on my own. He came into my life with help and financial assistance and over years made my ecological dreams come to reality. He and Nick are working together now so this great project continues on.

Here, I have to add a funny memory of Mum. In the middle of the tree-planting program, when I spent all hours and many days on the hills planting, my mother, in frustration at not being able to find me, left a message on my phone: 'Oh, Belinda! I know where you are – up

The results of all that tree planting

there planting those fucking trees!' I kept the message so every time my mum was trying to be a lady, I could play it.

I kept it for years, by which time she could see the funny side.

SAVE THE TREES, THE OCEANS, THE GLOSSY BLACKS – BUT CAN I SAVE MYSELF?

An attempt to save myself came with an opportunity to employ someone full-time. Enter Kate, the critter gal, an American who lived down the road. She moved into one room of the homestead while my mother was in the other end. I needed a booking agent and someone for location set-ups, though my mother did not need Kate's family of kangaroos, glossy black cockatoos and a duck that shat on the furniture.

Kate was an absolute godsend for me. Finally I had some help, but unfortunately the relief did not last. My mother did not like having her homestead turned into a wildlife park, and it set the stage for a slow erosion. Kate had to leave. My mother got her sanity back and I was left facing business as usual on my own.

If I was this cake of soap,
I'd surely have some fun,
Slipping down your sexy parts and soaping up your bum,
Sliding down your arms and legs
(Find places I'd not been),
Oh! I'd love my dirty mind
As I proceeded to clean.

I wish I was this cake of soap,
A rare and sensual joy,
To have at random what I please
With such a lovely boy,
And you would have control of me
Whenever there's a need,
To put me down and make me wait
To stop my lust and greed.

If I was this cake of soap,
I'd love the job and yet
The more you use me up each day
The smaller I would get,
So make the pleasures, we shall reap
Not often or too long,
So there will still be something left
When other things have gone.

Age: forty-five

It was at this point overload occurred, in the most horrifying way. Apart from all our ecological, creative and humanitarian pursuits on Kangaroo Island, my mother and I were now solely in charge of three dwellings for accommodation. We had no professional input – no accountant or booking agent or handyman or caretaker. My mother, now in her early 80s, did all the laundry, hence the name Turbo. She made all the sweets – 'Queen of Tarts' – and helped with the cleaning. My dyslexia reared its ugly head in trying to manage bookings. We had a sparse cleaning team with both of us always involved. Then there were all the location meals, the cooking and the set-ups, which were our new obligation to regular guests, now our best friends. Something had to give! It did. My bones.

I broke my wrists tripping over fig tree roots, my knees carrying two heavy pots, my ribs. Worst of all, a serious car accident while trying to avoid a kangaroo resulted in me being air-lifted to Adelaide. Doctors had to take a bone from my hip and put it in my knee cap to fix it, and screws and bolts were used to secure the shattered bones below my knee. I remained in a splint for three months. Did that stop me? No! I scooted around the homestead kitchen on an office chair on wheels to fulfil my cooking obligations. I also had a Buddhist monk, Pende, living with us and a country boy farmer who became my best friend (just to add to the mix). My country boy was probably the most uncomplicated and necessary part of my personal life. A Christmas gift I gave him explains it all:

DESPERATE

Desperation and anxiety have gone hand in hand during the hard times in my life – desperate to grow up, to leave school, to leave home, to get married, to have children, and then anxious to please, anxious I was not good enough sexually, anxious my children might get sick and die (Eliza did) and anxious that I wasn't a good enough mum (it appeared to me I wasn't).

Desperation and anxiety end in making decisions that are not always sensible. In my overload I sought professional help for Kangaroo Island from the powers that seemed to know hospitality. I flew over a couple from Melbourne who were big in the bed and breakfast hospitality business. They consumed all the *Fawlty Towers* information and then spat it out in a highly convoluted and complex form, which I could not understand. I hated the 'manager' idea so much that I rejected it all.

Then I began a serious spiral into nervous breakdown, culminating in my doctor finding suspicious cancer cells that needed to be removed. It was the first time I began to really think my body was breaking up and needed a break. My brain was in overload and this last health scare seemed to be warning me that I could die if I didn't take note of what was going on in my head.

Judy, my very good friend at the time (we always came together in crisis), was in mental health. I gave her a call while I was in hospital and she sent me straight to a cognitive therapist, David Coyte. He was my salvation. We should all have one of him. Someone who listens and assesses and then works on changing your programming and conditioning, sometimes affecting the true nature of who you really are. Chemical depression is very interesting as it can stem way back to long-term suffering that eventually changes one's thinking. I had to write in a journal every day. I was completely stripped of my false personality, replacing it with the real me.

Suddenly, I really knew who I was. But women still found me threatening. I still remained fake socially, but a few men especially saw me for who I really was. I was so grateful to find a way out of my dysfunction and I began getting out of my own way.

I wish I could say that, from that therapy on, I was like the phoenix rising from the ashes that then turned into a Whirly Bird and disappeared into the sunset, happily ever after. This was not the case.

The future became set in stone for my mother and me when she fell over in the shearing shed and broke her hip. Did she need a break too? There was no question that I would go back with her to Adelaide, as she needed rehab. Mum had a little apartment in the East End of Adelaide and it became obvious there was no other option but to persuade Nick and Rachel to take over the business on Kangaroo Island and for me to move in with Mum. It seemed the most sensible thing to do.

Mum and me on Kangaroo Island, before she broke her hip

A BUS TO NOWHERE

The decision to extract my mum and me from Kangaroo Island seemed a good one at the time, but I can see now I didn't give enough thought to logistics. I sold my Osprey rammed-earth house on the hill to Nick so he could use it as accommodation in the business and I had my bunch of old caravans with Marrakech as my squat and that was it. What was I to do?

One morning I decided I would get a bus, put it in an idyllic spot at Middle River and move around the island freely with my home on my back and live happily ever after. I was still in the East End at the time, so Mum and I literally got in the car, drove to the first caravan and camping outfit, and without second though, bought this huge old diesel bus for $25,000. It had been roughly redesigned with a kitchen, dining and bed area, but as I had no bus licence yet it required the owner to take it over to Kangaroo Island.

To cut a long story short, the bus was a disaster. It did not have the power to go up and down hills and the solar panels I installed dropped off. Once I had relocated it at Nick's Knob, I had no idea what to do with myself. It was the most ridiculous decision I had ever made. It cost me a fortune. The engine blew up, and it's only now that it finally has pride of place – at the back of the Yoga Shed. It has been turned into the Bollywood bus, decked out in Indian fabrics with a pressed tin roof and room to sleep for my two grandchildren, or adults like me who enjoy cubby houses.

REINVENTION

Nick and Rachel were busy as they had jointly taken over Hannafords of Kangaroo Island and changed the name to Life Time Private Retreats. They turned the Cliff House into six-star accommodation. Nick, Lisa and the children moved to Kangaroo Island, but it proved far too difficult so Nick stepped back and let Rachel take over. Over the years, they tried processing and reinventing new formulas with all their creative input but there was no one to take hold of the financial reins. I left them to it. I knew there were problems I could not fix.

There were far too many creative eggs and no one to sit on them long enough. It was only when Rachel's partner Sasha came on the scene things changed. They created a whole new business, called Hannaford & Sachs, and a proper restaurant and luncheon venue in the newly renamed Enchanted Fig Tree. I see Rachel now as her alter ego, Whirling Dervish, in her kitchen with her own personal kingdom on Kangaroo Island, creating pure magic as she whirls. And Sasha, the financial wizard, a warrior woman keeping the dollars on track.

Rachel

As wise as a Buddhist thinking
As quick as a dervish whirling
Like Queenie in her natural state,
Rachel keeps unfurling
As fast as a speeding bullet
As unique as a work of art
Rachel's a phenomenon
That dwells deep in my heart

My first thoughts about moving into the East End with my mother were for the good position and opportunities – and I had nowhere else to go. Kangaroo Island had become untenable.

My sisters had not been in my life in the years I spent on Kangaroo Island and, as for me, I wanted to be number one daughter still. But I found the pecking order was very different in Adelaide. I had placed myself in a position that I now felt I could not withdraw from.

I had demanded her love and she gave it back in her own special way. I did not want to lose a breath of whatever that was. I seemed caught up in 'doomed if I do, damned if I don't'. I was completely obsessed with our relationship because I did not feel I had an acceptable relationship with anyone else in my family. At least Mum needed me, and I her, and that was the bottom line.

In the first year at East End, everything was exciting. Mum had to decorate the apartment on the third floor – two bedrooms, two bathrooms, and a sitting and dining area dividing the bedrooms. We did movies and coffee breaks, I put on lunches and Mum reclaimed her old Adelaide friends with gusto.

Enter Liz into my life. A cook and entertainer, she was dynamic and divorced, girlie and fun, but we also had a like-minded connection relating to our mothers. It was a difficult time in that area for both of us and we were able to discuss these issues with honesty and compassion. It was also when I came up with the notion of 'a therapy booth'. I created the idea at the Old Lion Hotel, a little dark corner booth where we could download and consume plenty of red wine.

In between our family responsibilities, Liz and I travelled together. We were 'the two fun ladies' and had wonderful trips to Bali to stay with Liz's family. Our best and last trip together was to Olivetta in Italy to celebrate Liz's birthday – another chapter in itself.

New alter egos emerged. Liz was Principessa and I was Bertolucci, the photographer who filmed or sketched her all around Italy and France. My creative mind went wild and it was an absolute joy to share and travel with a person with a similar personal life. We both realised that a sense of humour could supersede tragedies and hardship.

Many years later, Liz has happily remarried and I am happily single, but we still make sure to connect on a regular basis and test out our laughing skills – and our truths, perpetually revealed.

It wasn't until my mother had a fall and broke her hip again that things began to change. Mum became very fragile and frustrated while I embraced the reasonably good idea to have time out to take a trip around Australia. I arranged for Jill to look after my mother and I ran away as far as possible. I had no plan. I aimlessly travelled, drove on the Great Ocean Road and ended up near Glass House Mountains at Chenrezig Institute, a Buddhist retreat. I helped the nuns paint the *stupa* and visited my very great friend Pende who lived on site.

The issues that still existed between my sister Jill and me were made even worse when I got back. I was on the outside and I couldn't wait for her to leave so I could get my mother back. Mum's disposition had changed in many ways. She was frustrated and anxious, and it seemed like all her joy had gone since the demise of Hannaford's of Kangaroo Island. There was no question that she did not want to feel like this. She sometimes wrote me a card to say she was sorry for being so grumpy. A hug would have been enough.

I have learned since then that there are insurmountable problems when family members take on a role as a carer. The main one is that a close and involved family member acting as a carer is more likely to cop flak.

Mum had a bell in her bedroom to call for me. It reminded me of the bell under the table at Robe Terrace to summon the staff. I felt subservient, substandard and solitary in the role I now owned. Funnily enough, it was Jill who instigated Mum's move to the Helping Hand Centre. Jill could clearly see the struggle Mum was having. When incontinence settled in and I needed to regularly change Mum's diapers, it became clear Mum needed a place in the centre. My sisters all came to the party and made it happen. I doubt that it would have happened if I had been on my own.

I Now Can Break Free

I now can be free
And truly be me
With no sense of grief
What a relief
A burden so great
Can now dissipate
No karmic debt
No things to regret
No selfish intent
No disrespect meant
No casting aside
And nothing to hide

I now can connect
With a certain respect
To a way to know how
To treat my mother now
Without her control
I have set a new goal
But with her in my mind
I won't leave her behind
But connect to a place
That will give us both space
So . . . I think it's grand
She's in 'Helping Hand'

Age: sixty-five

EAST END AND REIKI

To be honest, I did not feel the freedom associated with my poem. I felt responsible and anxious about my mother's new life at the Helping Hand and my life seemed on hold as well. Everything seemed outside of myself – daily visits, walks to the pub for a brandy, movies, and trips with Mum back to the flat for lunches that I put on for her and her friends.

At the same time, I needed help and direction and it came in the shape of John and Nikki Henderson and the practice of reiki. I had known John right back from the days of Jolley's. He was an intuitive counsellor and a reiki master. I knew nothing of the process but I trusted him when he suggested I give it a go.

It was life-changing. I found a new state of mind and felt my truth revealed. It also helped me reprogram my brain, which became sharper, and my memory improved, becoming better than it had ever been. I achieved my masters in reiki and joined John and Nikki on retreats up north and on Kangaroo Island on our property. I met a whole different world of beings. We all thought deeply, talked intimately and laughed heartily. I had the experience of camping in the centre of a 540-million-year-old landscape. It put perspective into my personal family turmoil. It was inspirational and I felt inspired to maintain the practice for the rest of my life.

Reiki is very specific and personal. There is plenty of literature on reiki and reiki masters who are willing to teach. Believing in body and mind therapy requires cohesion. John suggested I meet Gail, a naturopath, psychologist and astrologer. As one would expect, I had ongoing residue from so many accidents, with serious bone density loss and general body stress. Over the first couple of years, Gail gave me a preventative program that achieved more than I could ever imagine. It relieved the arthritis that had started to rear its ugly head. I am grateful that I had developed an open mind to natural assistance. I am convinced my little team will help keep me on track and expand my dimensions and beliefs for I have already learnt that there is more to life than what you see and hear.

Ahau

Space man, you know who you are,
Vibrations reaching from so far,
Galactic dreams, profound intent,
We know as Masters what is meant.

Trusting symbols that have force,
To stabilise, keep us on course
Humble thanks for all your worth,
That keeps me balanced on this earth.

CHAPTER 5

Digestivo

Digestivo, includes the sauces, a new beginning. They are the source of my cooking now. Today I believe 'less is best', and my kitchen reflects this with its one burner, a portable griller and a microwave.

These recipes are more for inspiration of how I developed a capacity to navigate thro hard times and provide an income for my whole life. There are no bad memories when I was creating food, eating and sharing. Enjoy using these recipes as a creative experience and have fun with them!

Nick and Rachel are still in the specialised market, and they fit that roll perfectly. What ever I did not accomplish as a parent, one thing I instilled in both, was a creative work ethic and they have both chosen to carry this forward in their love of hospitality. They will be able to pass on that part of a legacy I am proud of long after I am gone.

Fart soup

INGREDIENTS

1 onion, chopped
2 stalks celery, chopped
1 carrot, chopped
2 garlic cloves, finely sliced
4 mushrooms, chopped
1 L Campbells liquid stock
1 tin chopped tomatoes
½ cup pink lentils or Indian lentil mix
1 tablespoon sugar
Salt and pepper
1 tin chick peas
Weiners

METHOD

Sauté all the vegetables (chopped) in a tablespoon of butter or oil until soft.

Add the stock, tomatoes, lentils, sugar, salt and pepper.

Slowly cook on low heat for ¾ hour.

Add more water if it is too thick.

Add peas or chopped beans just before serving with wieners.

SAUCES

Tomato kassondi

INGREDIENTS

1 tablespoon olive oil
1 chopped capsicum
2 cups tomato purée
6 cloves garlic
Sprinkle cumin
2–3 teaspoons fresh ginger, grated
1–2 teaspoons sugar

METHOD

Sauté all in olive oil and cook on low for at least half an hour till capsicum is soft. Blend to a smooth pulp.

Asian dressing

INGREDIENTS

½ cup peanut oil
1 tablespoon rice wine vinegar
1 large shallot, chopped
4 kaffir lime leaves, chopped (remove vein)
Sprinkle of five-spice powder
1 teaspoon sesame oil
1 tablespoon soy sauce
1 slurp sweet chilli sauce
Fresh mint
Juice of a lime

METHOD

Gradually beat all ingredients with a fork or shake in a jar.

Quick peanut sauce

INGREDIENTS

1 large tablespoon crunchy peanut paste
1 clove garlic, crushed
1 teaspoon grated ginger
Cumin
Turmeric
½ cup orange juice
2 tablespoons coconut cream
1 tablespoon soy sauce

METHOD

Sauté peanut paste, garlic, ginger, cumin and turmeric for half a minute.

Add orange juice, coconut cream and soy sauce and mix well.

Tahini sauce

INGREDIENTS

1 tablespoon tahini,
Squeeze of lemon
1 tablespoon water
½ cup Greek yoghurt
Pepper and salt
½ teaspoon cumin
1–2 garlic cloves, crushed

METHOD

Mix tahini, lemon and water to a smooth paste. Add Greek yoghurt, pepper, salt, cumin and garlic. Serve with kibbi, chicken or fish.

Yoghurt sauce for fish

INGREDIENTS

½ cup Greek yoghurt
1 small shallot chopped
½ teaspoon turmeric
½ teaspoon garam masala

METHOD

Mix all ingredients well.

Yoghurt sauce for curry

INGREDIENTS

1 tablespoon olive oil
½ a knob (1 tablespoon) ginger, grated
1–2 cloves garlic, grated
1 tablespoon tandoori curry powder (Herbie's is the best)
1 tablespoon tomato purée
½ cup Greek yoghurt
1 tablespoon sweet chilli sauce

METHOD

Heat oil in a saucepan and fry the ginger, garlic and paste for 1 minute.

Add tomato purée and cook for half a minute.

Mix in yoghurt and sweet chilli sauce.

Quick béarnaise sauce

INGREDIENTS

¼ cup white wine
¼ vinegar
1 tablespoon water
2 pinches dried tarragon
1 tablespoon chopped shallots
Salt and pepper
3 egg yolks
150 g butter
Lemon juice
Fresh parsley or mint (optional)

METHOD

Put white wine, vinegar, water, tarragon, shallots, salt and pepper into a small saucepan over low heat. Reduce until half original amount.

Cool and strain. Place in blender with egg yolks and blend well.

Melt butter in microwave and only use the clarified part (the top). While still hot, slowly add to egg and wine mix until sauce thickens.

Lastly, add a squeeze of lemon and fresh parsley or mint if desired.

Sauce will keep in fridge for weeks in airtight container. It can also be frozen.

Lemon mustard chicken sauce

INGREDIENTS

1 cup cream
1 cup grated cheddar cheese
1 tablespoon hot English mustard
Zest of a small lemon
1 teaspoon cornflour

METHOD

Warm all ingredients except for cornflour until cheese melts.

Dissolve cornflour in water and add to sauce to thicken it.

Use for vegetables, or as an overnight marinade for chicken.

Peppercorn sauce

INGREDIENTS

1 teaspoon green peppercorns, mashed
1 tablespoon butter
2 teaspoons Dijon mustard
1 tablespoon brandy or tequila
Cream, lemon juice or Worcester sauce

METHOD

Sauté peppercorns, butter and mustard together in a frypan. Flambé with brandy or tequila. Add cream, lemon juice and Worcester sauce to taste.

Artichoke sauce

INGREDIENTS

2 eggs
3 artichoke hearts from a can, squeezed
1 teaspoon capers
Juice of ½ a lemon
Parsley and mint
1 tablespoon fish sauce
2 small garlic cloves
1 cup vegetable oil

METHOD

Place all ingredients except oil in a blender and blitz. Slowly add vegetable oil until sauce thickens.

MANY HELPING HANDS

A month before my mother's death, her physical decline became more severe and she was frustrated by her lack of mobility, but extremely grateful to me for paying her attention every single day. She had a softness I had never seen in her before. I was able to love her unconditionally, all memories of way back melted into nothingness. There was a world inside the Helping Hand Centre I embraced – I went to sing-alongs and get-togethers with the residents and often took Mum in her wheelchair to the local pub for a brandy. My mother was grateful and reasonably happy there. I got to know all the staff. Inner Mates were back to the fore.

My mother's physical aches and pains turned into a chest infection and eventually pneumonia. Every day I saw her, her physical being became worse but her tenacity was incredible. This was not the end of her. This was just an obstacle to overcome. It was a fight to the bitter end.

The fight went on for weeks and weeks, made more agonising by the fact that my mother was given nothing to ease her anxiety, no morphine and sadly minimal care. This was not the fault of the Helping Hand staff. There were just too many residents in high care with few family and friends. They did not have enough staff to go around.

My mother had got much worse. Her breathing was laboured, her chest was gurgling and she was on oxygen but she was not peaceful. She was agitated, trying to say something, nothing I could understand. I kept talking to her, right next to her on her bed, holding her hand and her head. For hours I talked about the past, trying to get her to relax, let go, anything to calm her anxiety. Eventually, in desperation, I called the sister to get the doctor who rather unwillingly gave her some morphine. They then sent me home, only to call that evening to ask me to come in. They told me she had got worse, but I found her just the same. It was night-time and there was no one around. I felt very alone in her room and fearful if something happened there would be no one to call.

At 2.00 am, Darren, my old favourite night shift nurse, popped his head around the door and explained they were in extreme chaos, as three residents were in different stages of dying. They were under pressure because none had family. I was the only one there for my mother. All the others were to die with only staff for company. Morning came with no change from my mother. I was upset, worn out and frustrated, especially when I was told my mother could go on for days. I rang Louie and said, 'I need an hour off. Could I meet you at the Buckingham Arms for a glass of wine and something to eat?'

One hour later we were sitting outside while Louie had a smoke and she suddenly stood up and said to me, 'Belinda, go! Your mother is being lifted up.' I scrambled into my car. Five minutes later and I was back at my mother's room to be greeted at the door by a nurse saying, 'Your mother has just passed away.'

I entered her room. Peace seemed to be with her. I really felt my mother had not wanted me to be there, but at that same moment, my daughter Rachel rang and made me promise to sit with her for four hours, following the Buddhist tradition of practices. I had to press the staff to give me this time. I filled the hours with listening to the most beautiful CD I had bought for my mum called *First Ladies*. I played it for four hours until they wheeled her away with a little bunch of freesias in her hands, which Mignon had brought in for her. They played the tune 'Hit the ground, babe, it's all right now, your eyes and mine, leave the rest behind, hit the ground, babe, and run.' Which was so pertinent to a non-believer of heaven or hell. Here she was taking off and running – into the fields of Kangaroo Island, maybe?

My Heart Belongs to Mama
(to the tune of 'My Heart Belongs to Daddy')

For Mum's eightieth birthday
When growing up with sisters three
Thru laughter tears and drama,
Nothing beats the party times
And the fun we had with Mama.

I have had my fill of feeling ill
With too much roast on Sunday,
But oh! She taught us how to cook
So my skills belong to Bundy.

So our skills belong to Bundy
She's the best teacher we've had
Our skills belong to Bundy
And that is why, we feel so glad.

All know her, from big to small,
For brain and style and glamour,
But when she's working on the land
Oh my heart belongs to Mama

She had no plan to till the land
But Dadda made her go
She's ended up a laundry lass
With a nickname of Turbo.

And when it comes to working mode
We know we are just students,
You should feel . . . muscles of steel . . .
In the arms and legs of Prudence
In the arms and legs of Prudence

Oh her muscles are really divine . . .
In the arms and legs of Prudence
So she can hang clothes on the line.

Our kids are wild about my mum,
It's really quite uncanny,
Of all the names that I may choose
The one they choose is . . . Granny.

Oh our hearts belong to Granny
It's a name that she doesn't prefer,
So our hearts stay strong with Mama
And Mama . . . is why . . . we love her

Age: fifty-three

AFTER MOTHER'S PASSING

I had lost my mother, but in the process I had become alienated from my children, my sisters, and my close friends. Family anchors had gone and social connections were fragile or non-existent, and that for me was the greatest loss of all. The dominant and all-consuming role I had held for the last twenty years (i.e. as a control freak) had been enormous, but hidden subtle effects. None I can possibly describe here. All I can say is, I truly had to try and get 'back to the source' and see what was there. There seemed very little. There was only the East End, my mother's apartment, the Helping Hand Centre. That world now felt uncomfortable to me. Gone was any sense of playfulness or naughtiness. Instead I yearned for hope.

There was now no job for me on Kangaroo Island. It was very much in the hands of Nick and Rachel, who put up a definite 'keep out of the business' sign. This is not a criticism. They had already had years of my bossing them around at Jolley's. Now it was their turn. But I did not take it at all well. I was upset and desperate, as I had hoped to be included in some way or another. I was also furious that my bus project had failed to launch.

Something had to change and it did. It came about through my sister Shylie. We had not had much to say to each other after the funeral, but at this extraordinary moment she suggested I sell Mum's apartment in the East End (which was left to the three sisters with the agreement that I could stay there while I was alive). I found out that I could use the money from the sale of the property to relocate and buy something somewhere else.

A miracle occurred. My old petanque mate, Chris Waterman, was dealing with rentals in the south-west corner of the city. He knew of a little cottage right on Whitmore Square that was owned by his mate who was willing to sell. It was a dream come true for me.

SARAH AND BERT AND BROOME

It was a dream come true for me . . . in a couple of ways.

Throughout all the family comings and goings, there was one person who was, and still is, constant in my life and that is Sarah, Shylie's oldest daughter.

Our relationship began back when she started boarding school in Adelaide. I was her continual support then, mainly because I had hated school and so did she. She missed her country life on Kangaroo Island. I would take her home for weekends. Since those times, my care for her had never changed, to such a point that it began to drive her mad! There I was trying to be her saviour because she was so like me.

However, when she met Bert, I stepped back and did not pay much attention until long afterwards, when they returned from Perth to live in Adelaide. One day, they asked if I would like to join them on a camping trip to Broome. They had already set themselves up in a caravan park with tent and trailer when I arrived with what looked like a body bag. The bag opened up as long as my body and was a metre high. I set up next to them on my own caravan site. Sarah and Bert could have tripped over me; I was so small in my bag. I loved camping. But I had never done it like this before.

It was very funny. I would wake up at dawn and peep out from under my cover and watch the legs of the grey nomads and hear the trundle of the poo trolleys on the way to the dump. Also, I did not know Bert very well, so I chose to dress and undress in my quarters – a difficult task!

We chartered a plane, rode camels into the sunset and ate and laughed our way around Broome. There was absolutely no 'three's a crowd' with us. We began our three-way relationship based on truth, respect, and validation of who each of us is. Philosophical and fun conversations were the key ingredients. Also, most importantly, it takes a very special man to merge with the two of us and know that it is about the humanness of us, not the male/female thing, which Bert really enjoys.

Meanwhile, back at Whitmore Square, my new purchase was in need of a serious makeover and what better way to extend our Broome connection than to get Bert, a builder and designer, and Sarah, in her alter ego, Builder's Bitch, to come on board. We knocked down the lean-to at the rear and built a truly magical room, with a silver pressed-metal ceiling and skylights instead of windows, which I call my 'womb with no view'. It is an all-in-one room – kitchen, living and dining. For a bedroom, I have a huge gazebo covered in greenery – a Whirly Bird's nest to sleep in and the best and most creative space ever.

Oomphstigumph and Builder's Bitch

Known them for years
(Three musketeers),
Family connections
Fanciful erections,
Mental inspections
Journal reflections,
Bertie the Bert and Serina the Singer,
Set up for a life of a Rich Hot Hum Dinger.

Age: seventy-two

That year of creative joy cleaned out all the old cobwebs and took my focus off Kangaroo Island. It also gave me a new perspective on life by creatively spending the money from the sale of Mum's East End apartment. Of course I ended up spending an extra $100,000, which means the family will be very happy with me when I eventually drop dead.

SYNCHRONICITY

In this new life at Whitmore Square, I have only one Inner Mate. This is Varda. She lives opposite me. We were both renovating our houses at the same time. Sarah, who was typing my manuscript and working as Builder's Bitch on my renovation, introduced me to her when she heard that she was a literacy consultant who flew in and out of Adelaide for work. When we eventually met face to face, I asked Varda if she would read through my manuscript and she agreed to do it when she went on a long-awaited trip to Italy. It was no coincidence that she would read my manuscript in the country I loved the most.

On return, Varda made one simple comment, 'Belinda, you must keep writing and get your whole story down.' From that moment, she came on board with me for the whole crazy ride. If it were not for her encouragement and persistence and the months of meetings, reams of paper and notes, I would never have reached this point. And what about her credentials? She is a Master of Language and Literacy, holds a Diploma of Teaching, is a registered counsellor and a specialist in behaviour and learning (she must have been made for me!). How lucky was I? I felt honoured that she bothered to take this long time out to keep me focused.

It was soon after we began working together that I realised the link, the synchronicity, in so many aspects of our thinking. Even sometimes when I wrote things down she would comment that she had often expressed that same thought herself. We had so much in common – our unique families, our love of deep conversations, our love of learning and being motivated by art, colour, gardens, people (especially the Inner and Outer Mates), laughing, analysing, and thinking and living creatively to name a few.

Varda oh Varda, just over the way,
We meet in the Kingdom, with so much to say,
The truth in the booth and the staff that we care for,
Give us a true message as to what we are there for.

Varda oh Varda, you believed in the 'Sauce'
You stirred it so carefully to keep me on course,
Friendship and hope are a part of our plan,
And I pray it will happen as much as it can.

RUNNING AWAY . . . TAHITI

Besides the Whitmore Square renovation, I was still in the midst of family dramas, with Kangaroo Island up in the air. Matters were unresolved in many areas. This is when I got it into my mind to run away again. This time to Tahiti! I felt like a bit of pampering. My choice was a small, classy, expensive liner called the *Paul Gauguin*. I loved the story of the art of Paul Gauguin and the Polynesians. I had been to Tahiti when I was nineteen, on my way to the United Kingdom.

Things did not get off to a good start. My luggage went missing and it did not turn up until midnight, just before our departure to Tahiti. It meant I missed the welcome cocktail party. It did not matter much as I was too petrified and upset to take in anything. I sat for hours in the steward's office and, for the second part of the night, I hid in the corner of the restaurant until my luggage was found.

The *Gauguin* is a magnificent ship. I had a beautiful room. There was luxury all around, including the restaurants and entertainment. But I was the only single person on the whole cruise and became aware, very soon, that couples and families are very reluctant to include a single woman on their table, in case they cling to them for the rest of the trip. I believe that not many people would have been able to deal with my feelings of anxiety. My first instinct was to book myself on every excursion and seminar available. That saved me. I learned so much about Polynesia, Marlon Brando and anthropology, flora and fauna. Even talking to people on the trips ashore, they never made any suggestion to catch up at either lunch or dinner. There had to be a solution.

Previously, throughout my life, connection with the Inner and Outer Mates had always helped. And now it happened again in all forms. The staff and captain invited me up to the bridge. I even got to dance, and listened to the personal stories of many lovely people. Uncomfortable feelings turned to relaxation and fun.

On reflection, I would not recommend solo sailing on small ships where there is little choice for company. Maybe some time in the future, my girlie Inner Mates and I can run away for a short time, but it will be for all the right reasons.

HELP TO SORT THINGS OUT

On returning from Tahiti, I had to face a financial and family dilemma.

I tried in every way to sort out my finances, which were dwindling

away. Professionals and my best friend and counselling lawyer, Bollo, could not accept the complexity of my accounts. Nor could I. I came and went to meetings that always ended in tears.

Everyone in the family, and their partners, were drawn into the mix, as well as Ian. It nearly destroyed us all. I realised that we were not the typical European family I had experienced overseas but a very creative, dynamic group lacking communication skills. No one talked to each other or had professional business acumen. I wanted happy families in our Kangaroo Island adventure and to add to this, Ian was trying to develop a tourist model for the benefit of our children, which I did not fully accept or understand. As I owned all the land, that was a problem, but I could not withdraw and my advisors would not let me, anyway.

It was very clear we needed intervention and thanks to Nick it occurred in an extraordinary way. Nick's mate, Hamish, could see all the suffering and introduced the family to an extremely skilled professional psycho-strategist and business coach. Enter Tim Dalman, who was prepared to save our family from ourselves before it was too late and with only the barter of Kangaroo Island accommodation as a trade-off in fees.

Tim met all of us together and apart, not for hours but for days. He flew to Kangaroo Island, gathered us up, and tossed us around with his special kind of salad dressing until we all 'got it'. I grabbed as much of his philosophy as I could. I just loved him and his intervention. His message was simple but extremely difficult to accomplish. Working together in business and trying to sustain family harmony was absolutely impossible. Rules and regulations were put into place, and no filtered conversations, emails or decisions were allowed without Tim on board.

As quickly as he came, he left. It was far too quick, as far as I was concerned. But fortunately he left in place a strategy and installed a close business friend of his to keep us on track and to direct board meetings. This was Tony Smith, a chartered accountant and business strategy advisor. Together we have created our code of conduct.

Artesia Pty Ltd

(Trustee for the N & R Family Trust)

Board Charter and Code of Conduct

———————

In this family business code

Commitment is the key,

Aim in separating 'family' from business integrity.

Behaviour is intrinsic in its source,

Transparent 'understanding' puts us all on course.

Accountability, reliability and objectivity is our creed
To achieving resolutions never based in greed.
In any code of trust,
Compliance is a must.
Ethical issues addressed at their best,
Lest personal interest is allowed to vest.
Family cohesion, is a fundamental reason
For the collaborative intent of all Artesian's.
United as one,
Including some fun!
Aim to agree,
Respectfully. B

This Code of Conduct and Tim and Tony's input into Rachel and Nick's business was all very good but, with that taken care of, I now had nothing to do. I was now isolated from the things that had been occupying my mind for the last five years. My reaction was to isolate myself even further. I shut myself away in Whitmore Square for weeks. The only contact I had was with John, Gail and Louie and I had two questions permanently in my mind, 'What am I here for? What is the purpose of my life?'

It was at this precise moment that something occurred, out of my control, that eventuated in life-changing repercussions for all of the family. It was nearing the end of the summer season on Kangaroo Island, Life Time accommodation was at its peak, and the Enchanted Fig Tree running at full pace with the Hannaford & Sachs lunches. Half an hour before lunch service, an electrical fire broke out in the service kitchen adjacent to the Tree. The fire took off up the hill, threatening all neighbourhood houses, then took a turn and swept around the beach and sandhills. Houses were saved but everyone's properties were burned. If it had not been for the Country Fire Service trucks and water bomber planes, all would have completely gone up in smoke.

Of course, the business had to close and everyone went into shock. Everything changed from that moment on, both symbolically and physically. Separation occurred everywhere, one after the other. Sasha left Kangaroo Island, Nick and Rachel saw the futility of trying to achieve family cohesion while their businesses were intertwined and they began to think about creating new pathways. Artesia, the code of conduct, the directors and the board were dissolved. After a decade of complications, autonomy rose from the ashes in the most extraordinary way. For the first time, everyone began taking care of their own business and control of their own destiny, and there was a reinvention for all in their individual exploits.

RACHEL'S STORY

Defining Moment: The bushfire on Kangaroo Island

A recent defining moment, which confirmed Buddhist teachings about truth, was a huge bushfire that closed my Kangaroo Island restaurant indefinitely. Mum asked how my Buddhism helped me cope, because as many other things were falling apart she, like most people close to me, expected me to fall apart. I remembered my lessons of impermanence – lessons that taught me that every object we find on earth is made of parts and does not exist independently, as our brain often tricks us into believing. I learnt that we cannot own things and take them to the grave with us, but that all things are unstable and constantly changing in a cyclic way. This is in fact the key to freedom.

'Freedom's just another word for nothin' left to lose'

Janis Joplin

On the days of the bushfires, everyone reacted according to how they deal with life and shock. The days of recovery became more about our own capacity to see things from a different perspective. I held on to my magical truth of the impermanent nature of everything. It was the basis of where my mind was. It was like a little natural shelter from wild storms. If I stayed in my truth, I knew nothing could really hurt me. I had my life intact and everything else seemed insignificant in the bigger scheme of things. It didn't mean I didn't cry and feel helpless at times but I was able to move through the shock more quickly and be effective for my staff, who were traumatised. I was also able to deal with the recovery and evacuation with some humour and openness and that is really the key to getting the most out of our humanness.

My strongest memory of the fire is when I was hugging my staff on the beach. We all thought my childhood house was burnt to the

Fig Tree kitchen after the fire

ground. We bid it goodbye, all of us knowing life is so much more important. When your heart is fully open (and sometimes that can happen naturally in times of disaster), it can become a moment you let go of ordinary thought. If we remain in a state of shock after these kinds of events we are not making the most of our oversized human brains, which to me seems a terrible waste of our potential.

Ashes

Empty trees, burnt from their leaves,
Empty skies where no bird flies,
Empty eyes in pain and doubt,
Wild life fearful, not about
Fire's fury, wind's intent
to change its course, from where it went.

But
Restoration will unfold,
That's what 'the originals'
always told
Wetness to re-seed again
Be inspired and wait for rain,
We have no power in Nature's
way,
And I am glad, that's all
I'll say!

Fig Tree kitchen after the fire

FROM OPULENCE TO EMPTINESS

Reflection and awareness led to a process of emptying out. I realised the opulence of Robe Terrace was behind me, and so too was my ego-driven desire for fame and fortune. I had financial security, but I also felt dissociated on all personal levels, and age was creeping its way forward. I needed a new form of acceptance. Unfortunately, I still felt anxiety and judgement from a family perspective, which I could not seem to break free from. I had to be able to get off the roller-coaster of running away or trying to fix everyone. These were not the true answers. The family code of conduct intertwined with Artesia and my ex-husband's input just did not work. I had helped to write the code with Tony and I believed in it, but subsequently I found it impractical. In any code of conduct, a manager or owner controls the code, paying his employees to comply. If they don't they are sacked. Not so with family, as I had already seen through Jolley's – had I not learned anything then or now?

It was only at this point that I fully understood the importance of emptying out control issues with my family, particularly Nick and Rachel. I wanted to manage others instead of putting a focus on myself, and it was this that stood in the way of my own progress. Anything outside of myself, I have no control of. Anything inside of myself, I have the ability to change.

I learned the Serenity Prayer thirty years ago and it has taken me that long to realise it is the most profound poem that has real meaning for me. I am not a 'serenity' type of person, so I have changed that word to 'courage' to suit me:

Serenity Prayer

Give me the courage to change the things I can,
The ability to accept the things I can't,
And the wisdom to know the difference.

Adapted from the original by Reinhold Niebuhr, 1951

Now I choose to connect with my children individually. I've learnt it is the human quality within us all that connects people, not their relationships with each other. If a family does not work successfully together as a group, it makes sense to me to build individual, loving relationships.

With Rachel, this has meant going back to the connections between us of Buddhism, yoga and travel, and our wonder in the nature of being here – the earth, the skies, the mysteries. Years ago, I named her Mercury, after the winged messenger of the Gods – quick-witted, quick-thinking, energetic, dexterous and perceptive, neither masculine nor feminine. That's her. No more the Whirling Dervish going round in circles.

With Nick, I have returned to our combined love of nature from when he was young, as well as our connection with his family and Kangaroo Island. Ecologically and artistically, the magician is still in him.

The fire on Kangaroo Island did many things to us as a family and they were all good. The phoenix has risen from the ashes in more ways than one.

I have my rewards too. I have returned to yoga and my interest in physical wellbeing. The music that Rachel created for my yoga practice at home has got me going again. I am back on track.

Emptying out is important. It is the pouring out of the residue of guilt, regret, obsessions, addictions and expectations. It is about cleaning out the subliminal anxiety that has plagued me all my life, and then digging deep for answers in the emptiness that seems impossible but defines who I really am.

Emptying out has given me a real opportunity to be creative and clear-minded, especially in seeing what is true and what is false. The process has taken a huge effort, a lifetime of journals, words, poems and sketches and years of cognitive therapy and mentors who still are helping me to go forward.

EVOLUTION

In 2015, I landed in my place in the south-west corner of Adelaide. The area is full of contradictions and has everything in the way of diversity. There are the artists who find inspiration in the local environment, students transitioning into a new life in a new country, professionals working in offices, and families all around me. I am surrounded by pockets of beauty and grunge, with a rawness and an ever-changing array of colour in the passing parade. Day and night, groups of people move across the central area known as Whitmore Square. The homeless find their way to welfare services for meals and shelter while others cross the square on their way to restaurants and cafés in the Central Market precinct. There are eclectic locals, and originals who congregate around St Luke's Church. There's a multi-cultural flavour amongst the students playing basketball, and unseen creators working away in little back rooms, as well as millennials at the newly renovated pub, Sparkke at the Whitmore, with its focus on diversity. How lucky am I to be a part of it all? I no longer need to travel far to find the Inner and Outer Mates: they are right outside my door en masse.

Looking back over my life, the one thing that stands out is the always present Inner and Outer Mates. They were there as household help in my opulent days at Robe Terrace. As a child, I felt sorry for these newly arrived immigrants to Australia. They spoke strange languages and were so gracious as they were bossed around by my parents. My curiosity was aroused when I heard their stories of history and culture. As time went on and the English of these Inner and Outer Mates improved, my personal interaction with them translated into something more profound. It eventually expanded to my life of travel, developing a sense of real friendships with others from a different social standing and even to foreign boyfriends wherever I went in the world. Those relationships came with no expectations, timelines or disappointments – just beautiful hellos and wistful goodbyes. The Inner and Outer Mates were never short in number and continually expanded my understanding of humanity in many cultural contexts. They are still a big part of my life today.

What else matters? Throughout my many life lessons, I learnt that it was very important to approach each encounter with curiosity and to practice going within for regular personal inspections while exploring outside to expand my experiences and mind. My home in the south-west corner of Adelaide provides the rich topping to my human cake.

A song I wrote in the 1970s says it all in the last verse:

Mind needs to ponder
I need a way
Encompass the feelings
Meant for today
Locked in this madness
I'll always know how
To never say 'Always'
But 'only for now'.

As I sit on my little porch shielded by six metres of garden jungle, which forms a natural barrier to traffic noises and voices, I realise that this is the most creative blank canvas I have ever had – it's a microcosm of my whole life all in a few square metres.

I am the Whirly Bird who has landed over Whitmore Square.

My home and canvas is defined in spaces. The first space is the boudoir, a Moroccan riad complete with a wall of fantasy dress-ups fit for my alter ego Figalinda and waiting so patiently to be worn again.

The ballroom takes over the second space. It is a tribute to Robe Terrace days and is full of antique furniture and candelabra. There is a large trompe l'oeil mural on one wall depicting a gothic ballroom that goes on and on forever. In place of honour is a portrait of my mother – a charcoal by Robert Hannaford in the 1970s. I know that 'lady' in the painting. She evolved from Turbo to Bundy and I took her on journeys through Jolley's, Europe, Kangaroo Island and beyond. I am so grateful I got to know her the way I did.

The next space houses Whirly Bird's nest, complete with a gazebo bed, full of light and covered in trailing devil's ivy. Oh my, it might strangle me to death one day. A couple of wooden magpies, given to me by Louie in memory of Bridget and Queenie, look over me whenever I rest.

The final space on my canvas faces St Lukes Place. Here there is another small garden with a huge fig tree. This is my memory of Kangaroo Island. When I open up my garage door, there is my Inner Mate Varda's front door, which is a constant reminder of how this book journey proceeded. So many times I have left my disjointed draft on the planter box of her front verandah with a note asking 'Is this a rap? Wrap?'

Oh Varda, oh Varda
Come into my larder
There's more for us yet!
So let us work harder.

'Belinda, what magical seeds did you plant when you opened that tiny crack in my front door, inviting me to come on this extraordinary adventure with you?'

Sourcing the Sauce

Can take us off course,
Nothing is static.
Life is erratic,
There is no solution
To life's evolution.
Sourcing the Sauce
Is a final last course,
The topping, the taste,
The fill up, the waste,
The slowness, the haste
Let's keep on track
I'm sure there's a knack
For Sourcing the Sauce.

Last but not least

Thank you

To my family for being the way they were, making my story worth recording and giving me the opportunity to create my Inner and Outer Mates, my life force.

To Poppy and Joshua at Erb'n'Flo, Sturt Street, Adelaide, a special mention. They capture the real meaning of diversity. Their café is a dynamic gathering spot for secret whispers and the loudest laughter. Poppy and Josh represent 'Mates' at their very best.

The real rawness in humanity lies at the feet of Michael Chalmers, CEO of Café Outside the Square, 34 Whitmore Square, Adelaide. This café is an entirely not-for-profit organisation that focuses on paying it forward by providing support and other training and opportunities for those experiencing homelessness and other disadvantaged groups in our community. It seems I have been rightly placed in my life on Whitmore Square.

To those who saw my vision and believed in me

Lisa Hannaford. We wrote the first draft together in Sydney, over eight years ago.

Nigel Hopkins. He inspired me to keep going at the Cliff House, Kangaroo Island.

Frank Webster. A life-time friend who was the first to read the complete draft and gave me a thumbs-up with constructive criticism.

Meredith Dack, who gave us feedback when we were halfway through. Varda and I took both Frank and Meredith's suggestions on board.

Tim Dalmau. He helped our whole family (inside and out) and had enough trust in me. He found me a special friend and publisher, David Lovell, who sadly died just weeks before I would have finished publishing.

Varda Svigos, Wisteria Bridge's Narrative Consultant, who was the pivotal point in this whole experience. She took me on year after year, until the last gasp of writing had been recorded. Varda is very special to me and is an intrinsic part of my life.

To Varda's family support: Mike Polaroid from Rumpus Room Studios for his work with images, and Kyriana Fountas from Treehouse Psychology and Wellness for her feedback and insights.

It was Varda's suggestion to take my book to Wakefield Press.

Michael Bollen. The publishing of *Sourcing the Sauce* with Wakefield Press has been monumental in so many ways.

Margot Lloyd. She did the most amazing job of keeping substance alive while cutting out the crap.

John and Nikki Henderson and Gail Bailey. For training my brain and keeping it in sparkly condition for more vibes to come.

To my family. My love for you, Nick and Rachel, knows no limits. You both put up with the emotionally dysfunctional mother that I was.

Grazie to all those others …

'Grazie' goes a long, long way,
'Efcharisto', in Greek, I say
'Merci', goes to the elite,
'Hi' to mates out in the street.

Grazi, greenshades, one and all,
For half my life I had a ball!
And Ally Wally and the Groover,
Do you remember the Didgeri Hoover?

Thanks to Cohen's and their lot
Angie and Steve there's a warm spot,
There's some you win, some you lose,
Memories of the Geaky Poos.

Grazi family, wide and far
What a crazy bunch we are
But had it not been for this glitch,
My tapestry would not be rich

All those humans from my past,
All are first, no one's last,
My list of 'Greats' goes on and on
But memories last, as I move on.

Figalinda, Fantasy Pants, Whirly Bird, Griselda, Bewilder, BB

Belinda

www.ingramcontent.com/pod-product-compliance
Ingram Content Group Australia Pty Ltd
76 Discovery Rd, Dandenong South VIC 3175, AU
AUHW020915091025
417801AU00002B/31

9 781743 056912